An Integrated Microsoft Office Simulation

ISBN 0-9774611-4-9

Diane M. Silvia, Linda M. Viveiros

Published by
Business Education Publishing
P.O. Box 8558
Warwick, RI 02888

For more information, visit our Web site
at www.bepublishing.com

BUSINESS EDUCATION PUBLISHING™
www.bepublishing.com

Copyright

 **BUSINESS EDUCATION PUBLISHING**™

Skateboards, Inc. Microsoft Office Simulation
Published by Business Education Publishing

Authors
Diane M. Silvia
Linda M. Viveiros

Editors
Michael Gecawich
Kathleen Hicks
Monica Handy
Martha McGuinness
Joy Tavano
Lisa Wardle

Classroom Reviewers
Olivia Handy
Carly Paquin

TABLE OF CONTENTS

TABLE OF CONTENTS *(continued)*

SECTION 5: THE INDIVIDUAL PARTS IN THIS SIMULATION

Section 1:

INTRODUCTION

This section provides the student with important background information about completing this book. It is required that you read this section before beginning this simulation.

INCLUDED IN THIS SECTION:

1.1 Welcome to Skateboards, Inc. Microsoft Office Simulation

Skateboards, Inc. is an integrated Microsoft Office simulation. In this simulation, you will assume the role of a Microsoft Office Specialist for Skateboards, Inc., a new indoor skateboarding and rollerblading park located in the heart of Rapid City, South Dakota. Skateboards, Inc. is not only a skateboarding and rollerblading park; housed within the facility is a food court (The Skateboard Shack), big screen TVs, a pro shop, an arcade, a lounge, and a disc jockey booth to keep the patrons "coming back for more."

1.2   Who Should Use This Book?

Skateboards, Inc. is designed for students who are enrolled in a secondary level computer applications course that includes one or more of the Microsoft Office software applications in its curriculum. The simulation is designed to allow students to use and apply their Microsoft Office knowledge and skills in an integrated, real-business setting.

1.3   What You Will Need to Complete This Simulation

To complete all of the individual projects in this simulation, you will need the following installed on your computer:	
⊙	The Skateboards, Inc. Resource CD. You will learn more about the Skateboards, Inc. Resource CD in Section 4.
⊙	Any version of Microsoft Word
⊙	Any version of Microsoft Excel
⊙	Any version of Microsoft Access
⊙	Any version of Microsoft Publisher or an equivalent desktop publishing software such as Adobe PageMaker, Adobe InDesign, or QuarkXPress
⊙	Any version of Microsoft PowerPoint

1.4 Prerequisite Skills

This simulation is designed to be used as a reinforcement supplement for Microsoft Office students. The student should have a basic working knowledge of the following prior to completing this simulation:
- Microsoft Word
- Microsoft Excel
- Microsoft Access
- Microsoft Publisher or an equivalent desktop publishing software
- Microsoft PowerPoint

Important Note: The projects in this simulation are designed to be completed using any version of the Microsoft Office software applications. The instructions in this simulation are provided in a generalized format and are not specific to any one version of the Microsoft Office software suite.

1.5 Your Role as the Microsoft Office Specialist

As the Microsoft Office Specialist, you will complete a series of real-world projects that will allow Skateboards, Inc. to open its doors for business. By using your Microsoft Office software skills, you will complete business and financial documents, organize data, and create and design marketing documents, databases, and promotional presentations.

The projects you will be completing in this simulation will contribute to the success of Skateboards, Inc. and increase your competency and productivity using Microsoft Office applications. As you prepare for your future career, the skills you learn from this simulation will make you a more qualified candidate when seeking job opportunities.

1.6 The Skills You Will Be Using in This Simulation

The following is a list of skills you will be using throughout this simulation:

- Creativity and design skills to produce business documents
- Applying technical writing skills in developing business documents
- Accounting skills to develop projected revenue and inventory spreadsheets
- Presentation skills to design slide shows
- Decision-making skills
- Organizing computer files
- Integrating Microsoft Office software to complete a comprehensive real-world business simulation

1.7   Table of Projects, New Skills Reinforced, and Approximate Completion Times

Table of Projects, New Skills Reinforced, and Approximate Completion Times			
Project #	**Project Title**	**New Skills Reinforced**	**Approx. Completion Time** *(in hours)*
Microsoft Word Projects			
W-1	Write a Press Release	Formatting a press release • Line spacing • Text formatting and alignment	.5
W-2	Create and Design Letterhead	Using headers and footers • Creating a letterhead template	.5
W-3	Create and Design an Envelope	Formatting a business size envelope	.5
W-4	Create Price Sticker Labels	Using labels • Strikethrough text style	.5
W-5	Create a Business Memo	Formatting a business memo • Superscript text style	.75
W-6	Create a Skateboards Bullet List	Formatting using bullets and numbering • Sorting text • Customizing bullets	.5
W-7	Create a Skateboard Terms and Definitions Two-Column List	Formatting text into columns	1
W-8	Create and Design an Hours of Operation Sign	Using tables • Merging cells • Shading cells • Inserting rows • Formatting cells	.5
W-9	Create and Design a Waiver and Release of Liability Form	Creating a business form • Changing row height in a table	1
W-10*	Create an Employee Welcome Letter Mail Merge	Formatting a business letter • Using the mail merge feature with an Access database • Inserting merge fields	1
W-11**	Create a Vendor Letter Mail Merge	Using the mail merge feature with an Excel spreadsheet	1

*Project A-1 must be completed prior to beginning this project
**Project E-1 must be completed prior to beginning this project

Microsoft Excel Projects			
E-1*	Create a Vendor Contact List	Entering data into a spreadsheet • Formatting column width • Formatting text • Using print preview	.75
E-2	Create a Lessons Price List	Selecting cells • Formatting cells as currency	.5
E-3	Create a Music List	Sorting data in ascending order	.5
E-4	Create an Employee Average Age Spreadsheet	Using the average formula • Shading cells • Creating a custom header	.75
E-5	Create a Projected Revenue Spreadsheet	Using the division operation in a formula • Formatting cells with text wrap • Formatting cells as percentage	.75
E-6	Create a Pro Shop Equipment Inventory Report	Using the multiplication operation in a formula • Using the AutoFill feature	1

*This project must be completed prior to beginning Project W-11

Table of Projects, New Skills Reinforced, and Approximate Completion Times *(continued)*

Project #	Project Title	New Skills Reinforced	Approx. Completion Time *(in hours)*
Microsoft Access Projects			
A-1*	Create an Employee Database	Entering field names • Defining field data types • Defining field size • Entering data into a database • Using design view	.75
A-2	Create a Member Database	Creating forms • Designing/customizing forms • Using queries	1
A-3	Create an Advertiser Database	Creating a report • Sorting records	1
*This project must be completed prior to beginning Project W-10			
Microsoft Publisher Projects **(Note: These projects can also be completed using an equivalent desktop publishing software)**			
P-1	Create and Design a Business Card	Creating and designing a business card • Using the rectangle tool • Using the text tool • Inserting graphic images	.5
P-2	Create and Design an Employee Name Badge	Creating and designing a name badge • Using color fill • Copying and pasting objects	.5
P-3	Create and Design a Bumper Sticker	Creating and designing a bumper sticker	.5
P-4	Create and Design a Grand Opening Advertisement	Creating and designing a print advertisement • Creating and designing a coupon	1.5
P-5	Create and Design a Coupon Flyer	Creating and designing a flyer	1.5
P-6	Create and Design a Booklet-Style Food Menu	Creating and designing a booklet style menu • Inserting columns and guides	2
P-7*	Create and Design a Three-Panel Brochure (Extra Credit)	Creating and designing a three-panel brochure	2
P-8*	Create and Design a Boarder Birthday Pass (Extra Credit)	Creating and designing a birthday pass	1
*These projects are optional and are included as extra credit			
Microsoft PowerPoint Projects			
PPT-1	Create a Grand Opening Slide Show Presentation	Applying backgrounds • Applying slide transitions • Inserting sound files • Applying continuous looping • Using custom animation • Using bullets • Printing slides in handout view • Presenting a slide show	2 - 3
PPT-2*	Create a Banner Advertising Campaign Presentation (Extra Credit)	Inserting a table • Formatting tables	1.5 - 2
*This project is optional and is included as extra credit			
TOTAL APPROX. COMPLETION TIME: (Note: Completion times will vary based on skill level and extra credit projects)			24 - 30

1.8   A Note to the Instructor

This simulation is designed to be completed as an independent, self-paced project for the student, with guidance and facilitation provided by the instructor. It is recommended that the instructor become familiar with this simulation prior to administering it to students in a classroom environment.

Many of the projects in this simulation are designed to allow students to exercise their own creativity and document-development skills. Although there are specific guidelines and instructions the student must follow in completing this simulation, the end result of some of the projects will be unique for each student. Hence, some of the answer keys provided on the *Skateboards, Inc. Resource CD* will vary from the students' documents.

To assist the instructor in administering and evaluating this simulation, a variety of resource materials is provided on the *Skateboards, Inc. Resource CD*. Please consult the *"Skateboards, Inc. Instructor Resources"* folder provided on the *Skateboards, Inc. Resource CD* for more information.

Section 2:
GETTING TO KNOW SKATEBOARDS, INC.

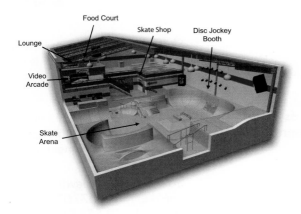

Food Court

Skate Shop

Disc Jockey Booth

Lounge

Video Arcade

Skate Arena

As the Microsoft Office Specialist for Skateboards, Inc., you will be responsible for creating a series of documents that are important to its startup. Before you begin, it is essential that you become familiar with the Skateboards, Inc. establishment. This section introduces you to your employer, Skateboards, Inc.

INCLUDED IN THIS SECTION:

2.1   The Importance of Getting to Know Skateboards, Inc.

Since you will be acting as the Microsoft Office Specialist throughout this simulation, it is important that you familiarize yourself with the Skateboards, Inc. company. Carefully review the background information provided in the table below to learn more about *Skateboards, Inc.*

Skateboards, Inc. Background Information	
Company Name:	Skateboards, Inc.
Company President and Owner:	Randy Boardman
Description of the Company:	Skateboards, Inc. is an indoor skateboarding and rollerblading facility that is housed with a food court, lounge, D.J. booth, video arcade, pro shop, and large screen TVs.
The Skateboards, Inc. Mission Statement:	To provide a state-of-the-art indoor experience where patrons can enjoy skateboarding and rollerblading and other entertainment in a safe, clean environment.
Address and Contact Information:	360 Jackson Boulevard Rapid City, SD 57702 Phone: 1-888-555-RAIL (7245) Fax: 1-888-555-PIPE (7473) Web: www.skateboardsinc.net
Hours of Operation:	Monday - Friday 3 – 10 pm Saturday 9 am – 10 pm Sunday 9 am – 8 pm
The Facility:	The facility consists of more than 30,000 square feet of total space. Eleven thousand square feet is dedicated to a state-of-the-art skateboarding and rollerblading arena equipped with beginner to advanced level ramps, rails, and half-pipes.
About the Customers of Skateboards, Inc.:	Customers of Skateboards, Inc. will consist of both males and females ranging in age from 13 to 25 years old. The majority of the customers is expected to be teenagers who have a passion for skateboarding and rollerblading.

2.2   Meet Randy Boardman, President and Founder of Skateboards, Inc.

To further your knowledge and background of Skateboards, Inc., read the story of how the company got started by Founder and President, Randy Boardman.

How I Started Skateboards, Inc.
by Randy Boardman, Founder and President

"One cold Sunday morning in 1998, I was out riding skateboards with my children, Randy Jr., Sarah, and Michael, at Rapid City Skate Park in downtown Rapid City, South Dakota. I started riding skateboards as a child and passed on the love of skateboarding to my children. I paid my dues on those cold, cement ramps. My daughter Sarah not only enjoyed riding skateboards, but also enjoyed rollerblading.

I had many conversations with fellow rollerbladers and skateboarders at the park. We chatted about how great it would be to have an indoor skating park that could be used all year long. On that morning back in 1998, Skateboards, Inc. was born. We were a small group of skaters and rollerbladers that rode for the fun of it, but I figured with just a little time and energy, and with the help of family and friends, I could build a successful indoor skate park. I discussed some of my ideas with a friend, who was a graphic designer, and before I knew it, he designed the Skateboards, Inc. logo.

I researched ramps and rails, pro shop equipment, and food court regulations and started looking for a warehouse that could be transformed into my dream park. I found a warehouse on Jackson Boulevard that was used for storage for a motorcycle dealership that had recently closed down. At that point, everything began to come together. It's been quite a challenge. I want to make sure that all of my family and friends know that this dream couldn't have become a reality without them. It's been a long, hard road but we're finally ready to "rock and roll" at Skateboards, Inc. – Rapid City's latest and greatest skateboard and rollerblade park."

Section 3:
UNDERSTANDING THE FORMAT OF THIS BOOK

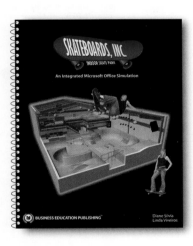

This section provides the student with information about how this book is formatted. It is recommended that you read this section before beginning this simulation.

INCLUDED IN THIS SECTION:

3.1   Understanding the Format of This Book

Projects in this simulation have been organized into an easy-to-read, self-guided, step-by-step format. The book is divided into five parts, each containing a set of individual projects for each of the Microsoft Office applications. For easy reference, each project has been color coded to coordinate with the Microsoft Office application being used.

A brief explanation of the individual sections that make up each project in this simulation follows. It is recommended that you read this section to become familiar with the format of this book.

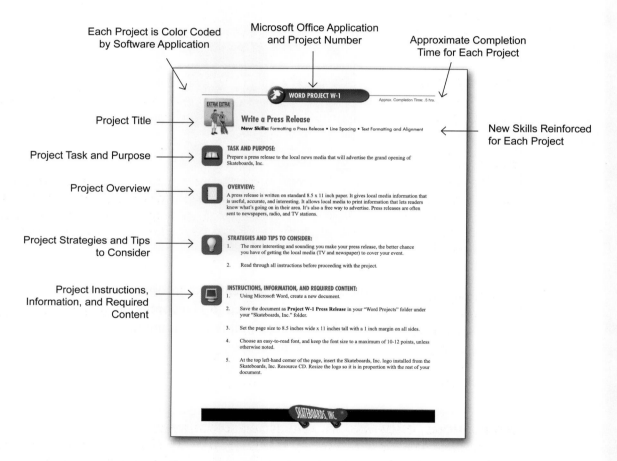

3.2   The Individual Parts of Each Project Explained

MICROSOFT OFFICE APPLICATION AND PROJECT NUMBER

This part of each project includes the name of the application being used for the project (Word, Excel, Access, Publisher, PowerPoint) and a project number that is preceded by the first letter of the application name. For example, the first Microsoft Word project is titled "W-1," and the first Microsoft Publisher project is titled "P-1." Note: PowerPoint projects are preceded by "PPT."

PROJECT TITLE

The title of each project.

APPROXIMATE COMPLETION TIME

The approximate amount of time it should take you to complete each project. The completion time may vary based on skill level and whether or not you are required to complete the extra credit Microsoft Publisher and PowerPoint projects.

NEW SKILLS

The new skills that are introduced and reinforced in each project.

TASK AND PURPOSE

This section provides you with the general requirements of the project to be created along with the purpose and objectives of its use within the Skateboards, Inc. park.

OVERVIEW

The overview expands on the information provided in the Task and Purpose section. It familiarizes you with the document to be designed and provides an explanation of the use of this type of document in the business world. It also provides an explanation of its intended use and purpose within the park. It is strongly recommended that you read this section in each project before beginning the project.

STRATEGIES AND TIPS TO CONSIDER

This section provides strategies and tips to facilitate the completion of the project, such as:
- Shortcuts
- Design tips
- Page layout tips
- Tips about the software application being used

INSTRUCTIONS, INFORMATION, AND REQUIRED CONTENT

This section provides step-by-step instructions to complete the project. It is recommended that you read through each project's instructions entirely before beginning the project.

Section 4:

USING THE SKATEBOARDS, INC. RESOURCE CD AND ORGANIZING YOUR PROJECT FILES

This simulation is designed to be used in conjunction with the Skateboards, Inc. Resource CD. This section provides:
1. instructions on how to install and use the Skateboards, Inc. Resource CD.
2. instructions on how to organize the project files.

INCLUDED IN THIS SECTION:

4.1   Using the Skateboards, Inc. Resource CD

The *Skateboards, Inc.* simulation is designed to be used in conjunction with the *Skateboards, Inc. Resource CD*. The *Skateboards, Inc. Resource CD* includes a series of file folders that are set up to help you stay organized throughout this simulation. The *Skateboards, Inc. Resource CD* also contains the following image files (discussed in section 4.5), which are available in a variety of formats:

1. Skateboards, Inc. logo
2. 3-D Sky View image of the Skateboards, Inc. skate park

 Important Note: The *Skateboards, Inc. Resource CD* must be installed on your computer prior to beginning this simulation.

4.2   Installing the Skateboards, Inc. Resource CD

Instructions for installing the Skateboards, Inc. Resource CD:

1.   Place the Resource CD in your computer's CD-ROM drive.

2.   Open the contents of the CD while in the CD-ROM drive.

3.   Copy the folder titled *"Skateboards, Inc. Simulation"* from the CD to your hard drive or network drive.

   Note: It is recommended that the classroom instructor perform the installation of the *Skateboards, Inc. Resource CD*.

4.3   Organizing and Saving Your Project Files

It is important that the project files are named properly and saved in the correct folders on your hard drive or network drive throughout this simulation. You will be provided with specific instructions in each project about how and where to save each file.

4.4   Results After Installing the Skateboards, Inc. Resource CD

After installing the *Skateboards, Inc. Resource CD*, you should notice the following folder directory structure has been set up on your computer's hard drive or network drive:

Folder Directory Structure After Installing the *Skateboards, Inc. Resource CD*

📁 Skateboards, Inc. Simulation

    📁 Access Projects *(All Microsoft Access projects should be saved to this folder)*

    📁 Excel Projects *(All Microsoft Excel projects should be saved to this folder)*

    📁 Logos *(see section 4.5 below for more information)*

    📁 PowerPoint Projects *(All Microsoft PowerPoint projects should be saved to this folder)*

    📁 Publisher Projects *(All Microsoft Publisher projects should be saved to this folder)*

    📁 Word Projects *(All Microsoft Word projects should be saved to this folder)*

4.5   Using the Skateboards, Inc. Logo and 3-D Sky View Images

Many of the projects you will be completing in this simulation will require you to include either the Skateboards, Inc. logo image and/or the 3-D Sky View image of the Skateboards, Inc. park in your documents. After installing the *Skateboards, Inc. Resource CD*, these files can be accessed in the *"Logos"* folder under the *"Skateboards, Inc. Simulation"* folder.

The Skateboards, Inc. logo and 3-D Sky View image files are hi-resolution, full color, and have been prepared in the following formats:

- EPS
- Illustrator
- JPEG
- Photoshop
- TIFF

Skateboards, Inc. Logo

3-D Sky View Image

The different file formats of the logos have been placed in their respective folders under the *"Logos"* folder on the *Skateboards, Inc. Resource CD*. For example, all JPEG formatted image files are located in the *"JPEG"* folder under the *"Logos"* folder. Prior to beginning this simulation, it is recommended that you explore the *"Logos"* folder to familiarize yourself with the different formats available. Consult with your instructor to find out what image format will work best.

Section 5:
THE INDIVIDUAL PARTS IN THIS SIMULATION

Now that you have familiarized yourself with the *Skateboards, Inc.* simulation, it's time to get started. The remainder of this book is divided into five parts, which are listed in the table below. Each part contains the individual projects that you will complete as the Microsoft Office Specialist for Skateboards, Inc. Good luck, and enjoy working for Skateboards, Inc.

INCLUDED IN THIS SECTION:

- Part 1: Word Projects
- Part 2: Excel Projects
- Part 3: Access Projects
- Part 4: Publisher Projects
- Part 5: PowerPoint Projects

SKATEBOARDS, INC.

PART 1: WORD

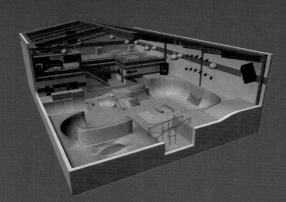

PROJECTS INCLUDED:

*Microsoft Access *Project A-1: Create an Employee Database* must be completed before
beginning this project.
**Microsoft Excel *Project E-1: Create a Vendor Contact List* must be completed before
beginning this project.

Write a Press Release

New Skills: Formatting a Press Release • Line Spacing • Text Formatting and Alignment

TASK AND PURPOSE:

Prepare a press release to the local news media that will advertise the grand opening of Skateboards, Inc.

OVERVIEW:

A press release is written on standard 8.5 x 11 inch paper. It gives local media information that is useful, accurate, and interesting. It allows local media to print information that lets readers know what's going on in their area. It's also a free way to advertise. Press releases are often sent to newspapers, radio and TV stations.

STRATEGIES AND TIPS TO CONSIDER:

1. The more interesting you make your press release, the better chance you have of getting the local media (TV and newspaper) to cover your event.

2. Read through all instructions before proceeding with the project.

INSTRUCTIONS, INFORMATION, AND REQUIRED CONTENT:

1. Using Microsoft Word, create a new document.

2. Save the document as **Project W-1 Press Release** in your "Word Projects" folder under your "Skateboards, Inc. Simulation" folder.

3. Set the page size to 8.5 inches wide x 11 inches tall with a 1 inch margin on all sides.

4. Choose an easy-to-read font, and keep the font size to a maximum of 10-12 points, unless otherwise noted.

5. At the top left-hand corner of the page, insert the Skateboards, Inc. logo installed from the Skateboards, Inc. Resource CD. Resize the logo so it is in proportion with the rest of your document.

6. Under the logo, key the following contact information left-aligned, single-spaced, 9 point bold:

    Skateboards, Inc.
    Your Name, Office Specialist
    360 Jackson Boulevard
    Rapid City, SD 57702
    Phone: 1-888-555-RAIL (7245)
    Fax: 1-888-555-PIPE (7473)
    Randy@skateboardsinc.net
    www.skateboardsinc.net

7. Double-space and key the following date left-aligned:

    May 15, 20___

8. Double-space and key the following heading left-aligned, 12 point bold, all caps:

    FOR IMMEDIATE RELEASE

9. Double-space and key the following introduction line left-aligned, 12 point bold, all caps:

    SKATEBOARDS, INC. ANNOUNCES THE GRAND OPENING OF ITS NEW INDOOR SKATEBOARDING AND ROLLERBLADING PARK

10. Double-space and key the following information left-aligned with a .5 inch tab indent at the beginning of each new paragraph:
    Note: Double-space the entire body of the press release.

    On Saturday, June 1, 20__, at 9 a.m., Randy Boardman proudly presents the Grand Opening of Skateboards, Inc., a new and exciting indoor skate park that has ramps, rails, quarter pipes, a fun box with stairs, and everything a skateboard enthusiast or rollerblader could ask for. "Having an indoor park will allow our patrons to have a safe, entertaining area to congregate and burn off energy any time of the year," said Mr. Boardman.

    Skateboards, Inc. consists of more than 30,000 square feet of skateboard and rollerblade ramps and includes a D.J. booth, large screen TVs, a food court, a lounge area, an arcade, lockers, and a pro shop.

    The day will be filled with fun, food, and entertainment. Andy Caron and Amy MacDonald (pro skateboarders) will be available to sign autographs. Each will give a short demonstration at various times throughout the day of how to use the different ramps, rails, and pipes within the facility. Our staff will also be available to conduct tours and answer questions regarding membership or any other questions you may have.

Come in and join the fun, and register to win one of the many prizes being given away, including a free one-year membership. For more information, call Skateboards, Inc. at 1-888-555-RAIL (7245).

11. If your press release exceeds one page, the second page should indicate "Page 2" in the upper right-hand corner of the page (right-aligned).

12. Double-space and insert the following three symbols (centered) to indicate the end of the press release:

13. Carefully proofread your work for accuracy and format.

14. Resave the file.

15. Print a copy of the document if required by your instructor.

Create and Design Letterhead

New Skills: Using Headers and Footers • Creating a Letterhead Template

TASK AND PURPOSE:

Create and design letterhead stationery that Skateboards, Inc. will use to communicate with vendors, customers, and employees.

OVERVIEW:

A letterhead is a sheet of stationery with the name, address, logo, and other relevant information of an organization. Letterhead is used to send business letters and other forms of correspondence. In this exercise, you will create a business letterhead template. This will allow you to type future correspondence into the template within Word, and print your letter complete with logo and information on plain paper.

STRATEGIES AND TIPS TO CONSIDER:

1. The purpose of business letterhead is to show others a professional representation of your business or organization, and to also remind your customers and vendors of who you are when you send them documents.

2. Keep the design professional, clean, and simple.

3. Stick to one font in the letterhead.

4. Since the logo is the most important element on a letterhead, it should be the largest item.

5. Read through all instructions before proceeding with the project.

INSTRUCTIONS, INFORMATION, AND REQUIRED CONTENT:

1. Using Microsoft Word, create a new document.

2. Save the document as **Project W-2 Letterhead** in your "Word Projects" folder under your "Skateboards, Inc. Simulation" folder.

3. Set the page size to 8.5 inches wide x 11 inches tall with a 1 inch margin on all sides.

4. Choose an easy-to-read font, and keep the font size to a maximum of 10-12 points, unless otherwise noted.

5.   Open the header and footer feature.

6.   In the header box, insert the Skateboards, Inc. logo installed from the Skateboards, Inc. Resource CD. Center the logo within the header box. Resize the logo so it is in proportion with the rest of your document.

7.   Switch to the footer command, and key the following contact information centered within the footer box, single-spaced:

360 Jackson Boulevard • Rapid City, SD 57702
Phone: 1-888-555-RAIL (7245) • Fax: 1-888-555-PIPE (7473)
Email: info@skateboardsinc.net
www.skateboardsinc.net

8.   Italicize the words "Phone," "Fax," and "Email" in the footer.

9.   Close the header and footer.

10.   Carefully proofread your work for accuracy and format.

11.   Resave the file.

12.   Print a copy of the document if required by your instructor.

Create and Design an Envelope

New Skills: Formatting a Business Size Envelope

TASK AND PURPOSE:

Create and design a business-size envelope to coordinate with the Skateboards, Inc. letterhead.

OVERVIEW:

An envelope is used to send a letter and/or other documents. An envelope contains the company name and address in the top left-hand corner (return address area) and the recipient's address in the center. The standard size of a business envelope (No. 10 envelope) is 9.5 inches wide x 4.125 inches tall.

STRATEGIES AND TIPS TO CONSIDER:

1. To establish a consistent, professional image for Skateboards, Inc., the design of the envelope should coordinate with that of the letterhead, with the exception of where the information is placed.

2. Obtain some samples of real business envelopes and analyze them to help you design your own.

3. Read through all instructions before proceeding with the project.

INSTRUCTIONS, INFORMATION, AND REQUIRED CONTENT:

1. Using Microsoft Word, create a new document.

2. Save the document as **Project W-3 Envelope** in your "Word Projects" folder under your "Skateboards, Inc. Simulation" folder.

3. Set the page size to 9.5 inches wide x 4.125 inches tall with .25 inches for top, bottom, and left margins and 1 inch for right margin and set orientation to landscape.
    Note: *This is the size of a standard business envelope.*

4. Choose an easy-to-read font, and keep the font size to a maximum of 10-12 points, unless otherwise noted.

5.   At the top left-hand corner of the page, insert the Skateboards, Inc. logo installed from the Skateboards, Inc. Resource CD, followed by the return address information shown below. Resize the logo so it is in proportion with the rest of your document.
      Note: Be sure to use the font you chose for your letterhead.

      [Insert the Skateboards, Inc. logo]
      360 Jackson Boulevard
      Rapid City, SD 57702

6.   Key your name, and your school name and address in the recipient address area on the envelope left-aligned. See **Figure W-3-1** below.
      Tip: The recipient area is approximately 2 inches from the top and 4 inches from the left-hand side of your envelope.

      Figure W-3-1

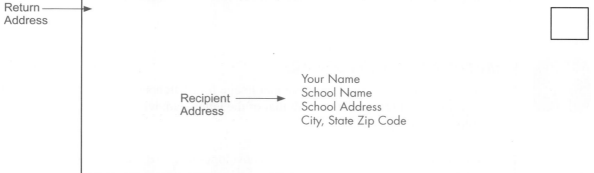

7.   Carefully proofread your work for accuracy and format.

8.   Resave the file.

9.   Print a copy of the document if required by your instructor.
      Suggested: Print on a real envelope.

Create Price Sticker Labels

New Skills: Using Labels • Strikethrough Text Style

TASK AND PURPOSE:

Create price sticker labels to be placed on the products for sale in the Pro Shop.

OVERVIEW:

The Pro Shop Manager, Kyle Logan, has asked you to prepare computer-generated sheets of price stickers to be affixed to the products for sale in the Pro Shop. He provided you with a list indicating the item name, item number, "List Price," and "Our Price" for each item. In this project, you will prepare four labels for each product on the list.

STRATEGIES AND TIPS TO CONSIDER:

1. Use your discretion as to the proper placement and formatting of the product and price information on the label.

2. Read through all instructions before proceeding with the project.

INSTRUCTIONS, INFORMATION, AND REQUIRED CONTENT:

1. Using Microsoft Word, create a new document.

2. Save the document as **Project W-4 Price Sticker Labels** in your "Word Projects" folder under your "Skateboards, Inc. Simulation" folder.

3. Generate a full sheet of blank Standard Avery 1 x 4 inch address labels (#5161). Your document should display a total of 20 blank labels, as shown in **Figure W-4-1**.

Figure W-4-1

1	2
3	4
5	6
7	8
9	10
11	12
13	14
15	16
17	18
19	20

4. Choose an easy-to-read font, and keep the font size to a maximum of 10-12 points. Use your discretion as to the proper placement and formatting of the information.

5. Type the following information in the 1st label cell block (refer to the label number sequence provided in Figure W-4-1). Format the List Price to "strikethrough," as shown below.

    Item Name: Pro-Tec Ace Helmet
    Item #: S7134
    List Price: $45.99
    Our Price: $34.99

6. Copy and paste the information above to the next three label cell blocks.

7. Type the following information in the 5th label cell block (refer to the label number sequence provided in Figure W-4-1). Format the List Price to "strikethrough," as shown below.

    Item Name: Bullet Knee Pads
    Item #: S2182
    List Price: $35.99
    Our Price: $24.99

8. Copy and paste the information above to the next three label cell blocks.

9. Type the following information in the 9th label cell block (refer to the label number sequence provided in Figure W-4-1). Format the List Price to "strikethrough," as shown below.

    Item Name: All Skateboards
    Item #: S9341
    List Price: $55.99
    Our Price: $49.99

10. Copy and paste the information above to the next three label cell blocks.

11. Type the following information in the 13th label cell block (refer to the label number sequence provided in Figure W-4-1). Format the List Price to "strikethrough," as shown below.

    Item Name: Salomon Rollerblades
    Item #: I2896
    List Price: $499.99
    Our Price: $399.99

12. Copy and paste the information above to the next three label cell blocks.

13. Type the following information in the 17th label cell block (refer to the label number sequence provided in Figure W-4-1). Format the List Price to "strikethrough," as shown below.

    Item Name: Skateboards, Inc. Baseball Cap
    Item #: S5221
    List Price: ~~$12.99~~
    Our Price: $8.99

14. Copy and paste the information above to the last three label cell blocks.

15. Carefully proofread your work for accuracy and format.

16. Resave the file.

17. Print a copy of the document if required by your instructor.

Create a Business Memo

New Skills: Formatting a Business Memo • Superscript Text Style

 TASK AND PURPOSE:

Create a business memorandum from the marketing director to the marketing staff advising them of space being reserved in *The Rapid City Gazette* for the Grand Opening announcement of Skateboards, Inc.

 OVERVIEW:

Memos and business letters are the most common types of business communications. Memos are almost always used within an organization. They are usually short, to the point, and do not have a salutation or complimentary closing. Memos have a specific format that is very different from a business letter.

 STRATEGIES AND TIPS TO CONSIDER:

1. Memos usually have a 1 inch margin on all four sides, and the writer's initials always appear next to the name at the top of the memo.

2. Be concise. Long sentences with complex construction do not belong in memos. Keep memos short and to the point.

3. Read through all instructions before proceeding with the project.

 INSTRUCTIONS, INFORMATION, AND REQUIRED CONTENT:

1. Using Microsoft Word, create a new document.

2. Save the document as **Project W-5 Business Memo** in your "Word Projects" folder under your "Skateboards, Inc. Simulation" folder.

3. Set the page size to 8.5 inches wide x 11 inches tall with a 1 inch margin on all sides.

4. Choose an easy-to-read font, and keep the font size to a maximum of 10-12 points, unless otherwise noted.

5. At the top center of the page, insert the Skateboards, Inc. logo installed from the Skateboards, Inc. Resource CD. Resize the logo so it is in proportion with the rest of your document.

6. Four lines below the logo, key the following text centered, bold, all caps, with one space between each letter:

   M E M O R A N D U M

7. Four lines below the memorandum heading line, key the following information left-aligned, double-spaced: (Highlight the initials after Rebecca Langford's name, change to a script-like 16 point font, and superscript.)

   To: Amy Reeve and Christine Stone, Marketing Staff
   From: Rebecca Langford, *RL* Marketing Director
   Date: May 10, 20__
   Subject: Grand Opening Advertisement

8. Double-space and insert a solid line extending from margin to margin.
   Tip: *Hold down the shift key and use the hyphen key or use the border or line tool.*

9. Double-space and key the following information as shown below, left-aligned, double-spaced between paragraphs.

   We are reserving space in *The Rapid City Gazette* to run the Grand Opening Advertisement for Skateboards, Inc.

   The ad will run on May 28, 29, 30, and 31 leading up to the June 1 Grand Opening event. I am looking for ideas and suggestions on design and content for the ad. Let's plan to meet next week to brainstorm and "kickflip" around some ideas. We'll discuss ad size at this meeting.

   What's your availability for Friday? Let's get ready to "Rock and Roll" and make the Grand Opening of Skateboards, Inc. an event Rapid City will never forget!

10. Carefully proofread your work for accuracy and format.

11. Resave the file.

12. Print a copy of the document if required by your instructor.

Create a Skateboards Bullet List

New Skills: Formatting Using Bullets and Numbering • Sorting Text • Customizing Bullets

TASK AND PURPOSE:

Create a bulleted, alphabetized list of various skateboards to be hung in the Pro Shop at Skateboards, Inc. The document will let customers know the types of skateboards that are for sale.

OVERVIEW:

The Pro Shop needs a list of skateboards they carry in stock to be hung in various spots throughout the shop. Your task is to create a bulleted list, then sort it in alphabetical order.

STRATEGIES AND TIPS TO CONSIDER:

1.   Read through all instructions before proceeding with the project.

INSTRUCTIONS, INFORMATION, AND REQUIRED CONTENT:

1.   Using Microsoft Word, create a new document.

2.   Save the document as **Project W-6 Skateboards Bullet List** in your "Word Projects" folder under your "Skateboards, Inc. Simulation" folder.

3.   Set the page size to 8.5 inches wide x 11 inches tall with 1 inch margins on the top and bottom and .5 inch margins on the left and right.

4.   Choose an easy-to-read font, and keep the font size to a maximum of 10-12 points, unless otherwise noted.

5.   At the top center of the page, insert the Skateboards, Inc. logo installed from the Skateboards, Inc. Resource CD. Resize the logo so it is in proportion with the rest of your document.

6.   Four lines below the logo, key the following heading centered, all caps, 26 point bold:

SKATEBOARDS FOR SALE AT SKATEBOARDS, INC.

7. Double-space and key the following information left-aligned, 14 point, single-spaced:

   Kryptonics Eagle
   Maple Bronze Series
   Chase CAB
   World Series Gas Chamber
   Birdhouse Completes
   Worldhouse Detention Deck
   Flip Appleyard
   Charger
   Ocean Pacific Longboards
   Sector Nine
   Tony Hawk
   G-Board

8. Select (highlight) the entire list, and using the sort feature, sort the list in ascending order alphabetically.

9. With the list still selected, change the spacing between each line to double-space.

10. With the list still selected, add bullets using the bullets and numbering feature. (You may choose any bullet.)

11. Carefully proofread your work for accuracy and format.

12. Resave the file.

13. Print a copy of the document if required by your instructor.

Create a Skateboard Terms and Definitions Two-Column List

New Skills: Formatting Text into Columns

TASK AND PURPOSE:

Create a two-column list of skateboarding terms and definitions to be used by the instructors during skateboard lessons to help patrons become familiar with skateboarding terms.

OVERVIEW:

Patrons of Skateboards, Inc. need to become familiar with skateboarding terms, especially if they will be competing in events. You will be creating a one-page, two-column list of terms and definitions. The list will be handed out to every patron of Skateboards, Inc. when they have completed their Waiver of Liability Form (which you will create in Project W-9 of the simulation).

STRATEGIES AND TIPS TO CONSIDER:

1. Read through all instructions before proceeding with the project.

INSTRUCTIONS, INFORMATION, AND REQUIRED CONTENT:

1. Using Microsoft Word, create a new document.

2. Save the document as **Project W-7 Two Column List** in your "Word Projects" folder under your "Skateboards, Inc. Simulation" folder.

3. Set the page size to 8.5 inches wide x 11 inches tall with a .5 inch margin on all sides.

4. Choose an easy-to-read font, and keep the font size to a maximum of 11 points, unless otherwise noted.

5. At the top center of the page, insert the Skateboards, Inc. logo installed from the Skateboards, Inc. Resource CD. Resize the logo so it is in proportion with the rest of your document.

6. Double-space after the logo and key the following heading centered, all caps, 14 point bold:

SKATEBOARDING TERMS AND DEFINITIONS

7. Double-space and key the following information left-aligned, 11 point, and double-spaced between terms as shown:
    Note: Bold each term, not its definition.
    Example: **180 Flip** - a 180 degree boardslide varial kickflip

180 Flip - a 180 degree boardslide varial kickflip

360 Flip - a 360 degree boardslide varial kickflip

50-50 - both trucks grinding on an object

5-0 - only the back truck grinding on an object

Backside - turns or rotations in the direction your toes point toward, so that your back is facing the outside of the arc

Boardslide - a trick where you lift your front truck over the lip, coping, rail, ledge, or whatever it is that you desire, and slide

Fakie - skating backwards

Frontside - turns or rotations in the direction your toes point toward, so that your front is facing toward the outside of the arc

Goofy-foot - riding with the right foot forward

Grind - moving along an edge with your trucks, scraping your trucks against the object being grinded as you skate

Heelflip - ollie, front foot goes to the toe side of the board, flicking the board with the ball of your foot, board flips, lands

Kickflip - ollie, front foot goes toward the heel side of the board, flicking the board with your toes, board flips, lands

Mongo-foot - a style of pushing where the back foot is kept on the board, and the pushing is done with the front foot

Nollie - ollie off of the nose of the board where you pop the nose with your front foot and slide your back foot towards the tail to lift the board

Nollie Heelflip - ollie off the nose (nollie), kick the board with the heel toward the toe side of the board with your back foot

Nollie Kickflip - ollie off the nose, kick the board with the toes toward the heel side of the board with your back foot

Nose - the front end of the board, from the front two truck bolts, to the tip of the deck

Nosegrind - only the front truck grinding on an object

Noseslide - sliding the underside of the nose on the deck onto a rail, curb, ledge, lip, coping, or whatever you want

Ollie - a jump performed by taping the tail of the board by which the rider becomes airborne

Switch-stance - skateboarding in the opposite stance than accustomed to, and passing it off as "normal"

Tail - the back end of the board, from the back two truck bolts, to the tip of the deck

Tailslide - sliding the underside of the tail on the deck onto a rail, curb, ledge, lip, coping, or whatever it is that you want to slide

Varial - rotation of board or body

8. Select the list of terms, and using the columns feature, format the terms and definitions into a two-column list with a line between the columns (the equal column width box should be selected). The width of the columns will be automatically calculated.
Tip: Be sure you apply the columns to selected text only.

9. Carefully proofread your work for accuracy and format.

10. Resave the file.

11. Print a copy of the document if required by your instructor.

Create and Design an Hours of Operation Sign

New Skills: Using Tables • Merging Cells • Shading Cells • Inserting Rows • Formatting Cells

TASK AND PURPOSE:

Create and design an Hours of Operation sign to be placed in a window or on a door to let customers know when Skateboards, Inc. is open for business.

OVERVIEW:

Every establishment should post its hours of operation in a highly visible area. In some establishments, more than one sign should be posted, depending on the number of entrances.

STRATEGIES AND TIPS TO CONSIDER:

1. Use a block style font to maximize the visibility of the sign.

2. Read through all instructions before proceeding with the project.

INSTRUCTIONS, INFORMATION, AND REQUIRED CONTENT:

1. Using Microsoft Word, create a new document.

2. Save the document as **Project W-8 Hours of Operation Sign** in your "Word Projects" folder under your "Skateboards, Inc. Simulation" folder.

3. Set the page size to 8.5 inches wide x 11 inches tall with a .5 inch margin on all sides.

4. Choose an easy-to-read font, and keep the font size to a maximum of 10-12 points, unless otherwise noted.

5. At the top center of the page, insert the Skateboards, Inc. logo installed from the Skateboards, Inc. Resource CD. Resize the logo so it is in proportion with the rest of your document.

6. Double-space after the logo and key the following headline centered, all caps, 36 point bold:

    HOURS OF OPERATION

7. Under the headline, insert a centered table with two columns and seven rows.

8. Select the table and, using table properties, change each cell height to .85 inches tall with the text centered vertically.

9. Key the hours of operation shown below in the respective cells in 30 point bold.

Monday	3 pm – 10 pm
Tuesday	3 pm – 10 pm
Wednesday	3 pm – 10 pm
Thursday	3 pm – 10 pm
Friday	3 pm – 10 pm
Saturday	9 am – 10 pm
Sunday	9 am – 8 pm

10. Insert one row below the last row in the table. Merge the cells in this row and key the following text in 20 point bold, centered:

> Hours change during school vacations and summer.
> Call 1-888-555-7245 for details.

11. Format the table to display a border around the table, but not each cell. There should be no borders between cells.

12. Shade various cells to make the information easy to read (*optional*).

13. Carefully proofread your work for accuracy and format.

14. Resave the file.

15. Print a copy of the document if required by your instructor.

Create and Design a Waiver and Release of Liability Form

New Skills: Creating a Business Form • Changing Row Height in a Table

TASK AND PURPOSE:

Create and design a waiver and release of liability form for Skateboards, Inc. that every patron using the park will be required to sign. If the patron is under 18, a parent or legal guardian with proper ID must sign in the presence of a Skateboards, Inc. employee or the form must be notarized.

OVERVIEW:

The main purpose and function of a waiver and release of liability form is:
> 1. to protect the organization and its members from frivolous lawsuits.
> 2. to make participants aware of the risks of injury in skateboarding and/or rollerblading.

STRATEGIES AND TIPS TO CONSIDER:

1. The only graphic to be used is the Skateboards, Inc. logo (installed from the Skateboards, Inc. Resource CD).

2. Since this is a legal document, it needs to be clean, uncluttered, and easy-to-read and understand.

3. Plan carefully so this document can be kept to one page.

4. Read through all instructions before proceeding with the project.

INSTRUCTIONS, INFORMATION, AND REQUIRED CONTENT:

1. Using Microsoft Word, create a new document.

2. Save the document as **Project W-9 Waiver and Release of Liability Form** in your "Word Projects" folder under your "Skateboards, Inc. Simulation" folder.

3. Set the page size to 8.5 inches wide x 11 inches tall with a .5 inch margin on all sides.

4. Choose an easy-to-read font, and keep the font size to a maximum of 10-12 points, unless otherwise noted.

5. At the top center of the page, insert the Skateboards, Inc. logo installed from the Skateboards, Inc. Resource CD. Resize the logo so it is in proportion with the rest of your document.

6. Double-space after the logo and key the following information centered:

   360 Jackson Boulevard, Rapid City, SD 57702
   1-888-555-RAIL (7245)

7. Double-space and key the following information centered, 14 point, bold, all caps:

   WAIVER AND RELEASE OF LIABILITY
   IF UNDER 18, MUST BE SIGNED BY PARENT/GUARDIAN
   (READ BEFORE SIGNING)

8. Double-space and key the following information as shown, left-aligned with a .5 inch tab indent at the beginning of each paragraph. Double-space between paragraphs.

   I understand that skateboarding/rollerblading can be a dangerous activity and that, by participating, I am taking a risk that I may be injured.

   I hereby assume all risks, even if Skateboards, Inc. employees or agents, through negligence or otherwise, are deemed liable. I hereby release, waive, and agree not to sue Skateboards, Inc., their employees or any agents, coaches, participants, sponsoring agencies, sponsors, advertisers, or others associated with the park.

   I understand, consent to, and authorize, in advance, the use of my name, voice, picture or other likeness, in combination or alone, in any broadcast, telecast, print medium, advertising, promotion or other account of any and all skateboarding/rollerblading events.

   I represent that my minor child is/or I am in good physical condition to participate in the programs and activities without jeopardizing our health. It is understood that I release Skateboards, Inc., its agents, sponsors, advertisers, and staff from all liability of any sort.

   The lower portion of this form must be filled out in the presence of a Skateboards, Inc. employee. If under 18, a parent/guardian with proper ID must sign the form in the presence of a Skateboards, Inc. employee or it must be notarized.

9. Double-space and insert a dashed line (or use the border or line tool) the width of the margins.

10. Under the dashed line, single-space and key the following information as shown centered, 10 point, bold:
    Note: *Include the parenthesis.*

    (Detach here)

11. Double-space and insert a table with eight rows and two columns. Using table properties, make the table row height .3 and set the cell alignment to bottom. Using a font size of 10 point bold, key the information into the respective cells as shown in **Figure W-9-1**.

Figure W-9-1

Name:	Address:
City, State Zip:	Phone #:
Date of Birth:	Date:
Signature:	
Parent/Guardian Signature (if under 18):	
Parent/Guardian Driver's License #:	
Notary:	Date:
Notary required if parent/guardian's signature is not witnessed by a Skateboards, Inc. employee	

12.   Merge the cells in the rows that require only one cell to display the information (as shown in **Figure W-9-1**).

13.   Center the text shown in the last row of the table.

14.   Format the table to show a border around the table and the cells as shown in **Figure W-9-1**.

15.   Carefully proofread your work for accuracy and format.

16.   Resave the file.

17.   Print a copy of the document if required by your instructor.

Approx. Completion Time: 1 hr.

Create an Employee Welcome Letter Mail Merge

New Skills: Formatting a Business Letter • Using the Mail Merge Feature with an Access Database • Inserting Merge Fields

> **IMPORTANT NOTE: Prior to completing this project, you must first complete "Project A-1: Create an Employee Database" in the Microsoft Access section of this book.**

TASK AND PURPOSE:

Prepare an Employee Welcome Letter congratulating and welcoming new employees to Skateboards, Inc.

OVERVIEW:

A welcome letter is done on standard business letterhead. In this exercise, you will use the letterhead template you created in Project W-2, add necessary merge fields, resave the template as a new document, and merge your new document with the Access Employee Information Table database you created in Project A-1. Your letter will go to all new employees inviting them to an orientation, tour of the facility, and pizza party.

STRATEGIES AND TIPS TO CONSIDER:

1. Your welcome letter should be short, inviting, and to the point.

2. A welcome letter should provide useful information.

3. Before you begin the project, you may want to print a hard copy of Project A-1 to use as a visual reference.

4. Read through all instructions before proceeding with the project.

INSTRUCTIONS, INFORMATION, AND REQUIRED CONTENT:

1. Using Microsoft Word, open **Project W-2 Letterhead** in your "Word Projects" folder under your "Skateboards, Inc. Simulation" folder.

2. To avoid overwriting your original letterhead file, save the document as **Project W-10 Employee Welcome Letter Template** in your "Word Projects" folder under your "Skateboards, Inc. Simulation" folder.
   Tip: Remember to use "Save As."

3. Set the page size to 8.5 inches wide x 11 inches tall with a 1 inch margin on all sides.

4. Choose an easy-to-read font, and keep the font size to a maximum of 10-12 points, unless otherwise noted.

5. Using the mail merge feature, set up the main document indicating "Letters" as the document type.

6. Using the mail merge feature, select the file "Employee Database" (created in **Project A-1 Employee Database** in your "Access Projects" folder under your "Skateboards, Inc. Simulation" folder).
   Note: This step will connect the main document (the letter) to the data source document; the data source document does not actually display on the screen.

7. At approximately 2.5 inches down from the top, key the following date left-aligned:

   May 1, 20__

8. Using the mail merge feature, insert the following merge fields four lines below the date left-aligned:
   Note: Insert the necessary spaces and punctuation between merge fields as shown below.

   «Salutation» «Fname» «Lname»
   «Street»
   «City», «State» «Zip»

9. Two lines below the address block, insert the following salutation text and merge field left-aligned:
   Note: Insert a colon after the «Fname» merge field.

   Dear «Fname»:

10. Two lines below the salutation, key the following text, single-spaced, left-aligned, and double-spaced between paragraphs:
    Note: Within the body of the letter, a merge field needs to be inserted for the employee's title.

    Congratulations and welcome to Skateboards, Inc. We are delighted you are going to join our team as a new «Title». Your role is critical in fulfilling the mission of our organization.

    Please join us on Monday, May 15, 20__, at 1 p.m., for an orientation, tour of the facility, and pizza party where you will meet all of your new co-workers. At that time, you will receive your orientation packet which will include all of the rules and regulations, membership information, waiver for riders, and other essential information.

    We are looking forward to a long-term relationship and your success at Skateboards, Inc. Thank you for choosing to join our team.

11. Double-space and key the following closing left-aligned:

   Sincerely,

12. Four lines below the closing, key the following text left-aligned:

   Randy Boardman
   President

13. Carefully proofread your work for accuracy and format.

14. Resave the file.

15. Print a copy if required by your instructor.

16. Using the mail merge feature, merge your letters to a new document.

17. Carefully proofread your work for accuracy and format.

18. Save the document as **Project W-10 Employee Welcome Letter Merged** in your "Word Projects" folder under your "Skateboards, Inc. Simulation" folder.

19. Print a copy of one or more of the merged letters if required by your instructor.

Create a Vendor Letter Mail Merge

New Skills: Using the Mail Merge Feature with an Excel Spreadsheet

IMPORTANT NOTE: Prior to completing this project, you must first complete "Project E-1: Create a Vendor Contact List" in the Microsoft Excel section of this book.

TASK AND PURPOSE:

Create a letter to the vendors of Skateboards, Inc. providing them with the opportunity to promote their products to members and guests at the Grand Opening Celebration on June 1, 20__.

OVERVIEW:

Vendors often seek new and creative ways to promote their products or services. Sometimes they provide door prizes (such as samples of the products they have for sale), or promotional buttons, pins, or pens depicting their company logo or slogan. At times, groups, organizations, and businesses work together to promote their respective interests. In this exercise, you will use the letterhead template you created in Project W-2, add necessary merge fields, resave the template as a new document, and merge your new document with the Vendor Contact List you created in Project E-1.

STRATEGIES AND TIPS TO CONSIDER:

1. Business communications should be brief, easy-to-read, and clearly state the intended message.

2. Before you begin the project, you may want to print a hard copy of the data source document to have as a visual reference.

3. Read through all instructions before proceeding with the project.

INSTRUCTIONS, INFORMATION, AND REQUIRED CONTENT:

1. Using Microsoft Word, open **Project W-2 Letterhead** in your "Word Projects" folder under your "Skateboards, Inc. Simulation" folder.

2. To avoid overwriting your original letterhead file, save the document as **Project W-11 Vendor Letter Template** in your "Word Projects" folder under your "Skateboards, Inc. Simulation" folder.
    Tip: Remember to use "Save As."

3. Set the page size to 8.5 inches wide x 11 inches tall with a 1 inch margin on all sides.

4. Choose an easy-to-read font, and keep the font size to a maximum of 10-12 points, unless otherwise noted.

5. Using the mail merge feature, set up the main document indicating "Letters" as the document type.

6. Using the mail merge feature, select the file "Vendor Contact List" (created in **Project E-1 Vendor Contact List** in your "Excel Projects" folder under your "Skateboards, Inc. Simulation" folder).
    Note: This step will connect the main document (the letter) to the data source document; the data source document does not actually display on the screen.

7. At approximately 2.5 inches down from the top, key the following date left-aligned:

    May 15, 20__

8. Using the mail merge feature, insert the following merge fields four lines below the date left-aligned:
    Note: Insert the necessary spaces and punctuation between merge fields as shown below.

    «VendorName»
    «Street»
    «City», «State» «Zip»

9. Double-space and key the following letter, single-spaced, left-aligned, and double-spaced between paragraphs:
    Note: Within the body of the letter, a merge field needs to be inserted for the Vendor Name in the first and last paragraphs.

    To Whom It May Concern:

    The management team at Skateboards, Inc. is pleased to establish a relationship with «VendorName», and we look forward to doing business with you.

    Our Grand Opening Celebration will take place on June 1, 20__. We invite you to participate in our celebration and extend to you an opportunity to promote your products or services in a number of ways at the event. For instance, your company could donate a "door prize," such as a gift certificate to be given away during the celebration, or contribute promotional items (pens, buttons, key chains, pins) depicting your company logo or slogan to be distributed to our guests.

    Please let us know by return mail whether you plan to participate and the nature and quantity of items to be contributed.

We look forward to celebrating our Grand Opening with a representative of «VendorName» and to promoting your products and services.

Sincerely,

Randy Boardman
President

10. Carefully proofread your work for accuracy and format.

11. Resave the file.

12. Print a copy if required by your instructor.

13. Using the mail merge feature, merge your letters to a new document.
    Note: *When prompted to merge the documents, set the range to merge records 1 to 20.*

14. Carefully proofread your work for accuracy and format.

15. Save the document as **Project W-11 Vendor Letter Merged** in your "Word Projects" folder under your "Skateboards, Inc. Simulation" folder.

16. Print a copy of one or more of the merged letters if required by your instructor.

SKATEBOARDS, INC.

PART 2:
EXCEL

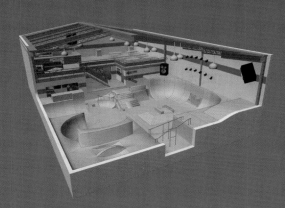

PROJECTS INCLUDED:

*This project must be completed before beginning Microsoft Word *Project W-11: Vendor Letter Mail Merge*.

Create a Vendor Contact List

New Skills: Entering Data into a Spreadsheet • Formatting Column Width • Formatting Text
• Using Print Preview

> **IMPORTANT NOTE:** This project must be completed prior to beginning
> "Project W-11: Create a Vendor Letter Mail Merge" in the Microsoft Word section of this book.

TASK AND PURPOSE:

Create a vendor list for Skateboards, Inc. that includes vendor name, address, and telephone number. This list will be used for communication with vendors.

OVERVIEW:

Businesses contact vendors to inquire about new and existing products, discuss methods of shipment and terms of payment, and ascertain the status of orders. Maintaining an accurate, up-to-date vendor list is essential.

STRATEGIES AND TIPS TO CONSIDER:

1. Whenever you create a database or a spreadsheet, be consistent in the manner in which you input the data. For instance, "S.D." should be consistently entered as "S.D." not "SD." Consistent data entry will ensure accurate results if you need to filter or sort the data by category at a later time.

2. Read through all instructions before proceeding with the project.

INSTRUCTIONS, INFORMATION, AND REQUIRED CONTENT:

1. Using Microsoft Excel, create a new blank workbook.

2. Save the document as **Project E-1 Vendor Contact List** in your "Excel Projects" folder under your "Skateboards, Inc. Simulation" folder.

3. Format the width of column A to 32, B to 22, C to 12, D and E to 6, and F to 15.

4. Key the data as it appears in **Figure E-1-1** into the spreadsheet. Unless otherwise noted, the font should be set to Arial 10 point.

5. Format cells A1 – F1 as bold.

6. Carefully proofread your work for accuracy and format.

7. Resave the file.

8. Set the Print Area to include all cells containing data in the spreadsheet.

9. Print Preview and adjust the Page Setup so that the spreadsheet fits on one page.

10. Print a copy of the document if required by your instructor.

Figure E-1-1

	A	B	C	D	E	F
1	VendorName	Street	City	State	Zip	Telephone
2	Ace Book Company	39 Harrison Avenue	Philadelphia	PA	19092	215-689-4412
3	Badlands Janitorial Supplies	36 Water Street	Rapid City	SD	57703	605-333-5269
4	Black Hills Food & Beverage Supply	15 Bluepoint Road	Spearfish	SD	57783	605-324-7982
5	Bullet, Inc.	122 Chestnut Street	Hot Springs	SD	57747	605-411-3919
6	Cheyenne River Office Supply	57 Hathaway Avenue	Mobridge	SD	57601	605-429-6817
7	Clear Lake Electronics	2 Tyler Road	Clear Lake	SD	57226	605-317-7196
8	Custom Decals Co.	208 William Street	Los Angeles	CA	90005	213-792-5680
9	Deathbox, Inc.	52 Pleasant Street	Aberdeen	SD	57401	605-812-5411
10	Destructo, Inc.	782 Point Road	Denver	CO	80014	800-264-3000
11	Magazines Unlimited	1582 Rutherford Avenue	Rapid City	SD	57703	605-436-1122
12	Motto, Inc.	259 Seventh Avenue	New York	NY	10002	212-514-6678
13	Mt. Rushmore Game Products	12 Middle Road	Rapid City	SD	57703	605-382-3855
14	Pro-Tec Supply	30 Highland Road	Boston	MA	02103	617-963-5143
15	Salomon	12 Hoxey Road	Rapid City	SD	57703	605-373-0931
16	Speed Demon	402 Alley Road	Aberdeen	SD	57401	605-444-2688
17	Sport Caps Company	12 Clearview Avenue	Miami	FL	33013	305-763-9968
18	Topspeed Enterprises	12 Oxford Avenue	Park City	UT	84060	888-462-7100
19	Wheeling Clothing Co.	147 Liberty Street	Minneapolis	MN	55404	612-347-1900
20	Wind Cave Music	302 Pine Lake Road	Watertown	SD	57735	605-692-1184

Create a Lessons Price List

New Skills: Selecting Cells • Formatting Cells as Currency

TASK AND PURPOSE:

Create a Lessons Price List that shows the cost of private and group skateboarding lessons offered by Skateboards, Inc.

OVERVIEW:

Skateboards, Inc. has hired a team of top-notch skateboarding instructors for both private and group skateboarding lessons. The spreadsheet you create will outline the cost of private and group lessons.

STRATEGIES AND TIPS TO CONSIDER:

1. This is an internal spreadsheet. Keep it simple. No graphics are necessary.

2. Read through all instructions before proceeding with the project.

INSTRUCTIONS, INFORMATION, AND REQUIRED CONTENT:

1. Using Microsoft Excel, create a new blank workbook.

2. Save the document as **Project E-2 Lessons Price List** in your "Excel Projects" folder under your "Skateboards, Inc. Simulation" folder.

3. Format the width of column A to 52 and column B to 15.

4. Key the data as it appears in **Figure E-2-1** into the spreadsheet. Unless otherwise noted, the font should be set to Arial 10 point.

5. Change the font size of cell A1 to 12 point.

6. Select and format cells A1, A3, A6, A8, and A12 as bold.
    Tip: Hold down the control key as you click on each cell.

7. Select cells B4 – B16 and format them as currency with 0 decimal places and display the $ symbol.

8. Format cell A18 as italic.

9.   Carefully proofread your work for accuracy and format.

10.   Resave the file.

11.   Set the Print Area to include all cells containing data in the spreadsheet.

12.   Print Preview and adjust the Page Setup so that the spreadsheet fits on one page.

13.   Print a copy of the document if required by your instructor.

Figure E-2-1

	A	B
1	SKATEBOARDS, INC. LESSONS PRICE LIST	
2		
3	Enrollment Fee:	
4	Single Student	35
5	Group (per student)	30
6	Private Lesson:	
7	1 student	60
8	Group Lesson:	
9	2 students	75
10	3 students	90
11	4 or more students (per person)	25
12	Package Deals (includes Enrollment Fee and Lessons):	
13	Package 1 (1 lesson)	80
14	Package 2 (2 lessons)	130
15	Package 3 (3 lessons)	180
16	Package 4 (4 lessons)	225
17		
18	Note: All lessons consist of one hour of instruction	

Create a Music List

New Skills: Sorting Data in Ascending Order

TASK AND PURPOSE:

Create a Music List for the D.J. Booth at Skateboards, Inc. Patrons renting the park for special events will have the opportunity to request their favorite songs, artists, or music type. Listening to their favorite music will enhance the fun and excitement of the special event.

OVERVIEW:

The Music List will provide the name of the song or music piece, the artist, and the music type. In the process of booking reservations for special functions to be held at Skateboards, Inc., management will advise renters that they may request specific music for their event by contacting D.J. Jazz at the Music Booth. D.J. Jazz will present the Music List to the renters and have them select specific songs, artists, or types of music (country, jazz, pop, rhythm and blues, rap, rock & roll) to be played at their event.

STRATEGIES AND TIPS TO CONSIDER:

1. Whenever you create a spreadsheet, be consistent in the manner in which you input the data. For instance, "Rock & Roll" should consistently be entered as "Rock & Roll," not "Rock and Roll." Consistent data entry will ensure accurate results if you need to filter or sort the data by category at a later time.

2. Read through all instructions before proceeding with the project.

INSTRUCTIONS, INFORMATION, AND REQUIRED CONTENT:

1. Using Microsoft Excel, create a new blank workbook.

2. Save the document as **Project E-3 Music List** in your "Excel Projects" folder under your "Skateboards, Inc. Simulation" folder.

3. Format the width of column A to 25, and columns B and C to 20.

4. Key the data as it appears in **Figure E-3-1** into the spreadsheet. Unless otherwise noted, the font should be set to Arial 10 point.

5. Format cell A1 to 14 point bold.

6. Bold and center align cells A3 – C3.

7. Sort the data in the spreadsheet by "Music Type" in ascending order.

8. Carefully proofread your work for accuracy and format.

9. Resave the file.

10. Set the Print Area to include all cells containing data in the spreadsheet.

11. Print Preview and adjust the Page Setup so that the spreadsheet fits on one page.

12. Print a copy of the document if required by your instructor.

Figure E-3-1

	A	B	C
1	D.J. Jazz Sample Music List - Skateboards, Inc.		
2			
3	Name of Song	Artist	Music Type
4	Heels Over Head	Crazy Davy	Country
5	Spinning	Jonesy	Jazz
6	Don't Give Up!	Johnny Steele	Pop
7	Cruisin'	Sammy Toolis	Rhythm & Blues
8	Go For It!	The Upbeats	Pop
9	It's So Easy	Pressure	Pop
10	Flyin' High	Aces High	Rhythm & Blues
11	100 Ways	Kaleidescope	Rock & Roll
12	Turning Point	Country Boys	Country
13	Keep on Tryin'	Timmy Z	Rap
14	Rolling on Down the Track	Musicmaker	Rhythm & Blues
15	Let's Go Crazy	Blitz	Rock & Roll
16	Footloose	Ken Lang	Country
17	Wheels A-Turnin'	Melissa Marlow	Rhythm & Blues
18	Maniac	Michael Lewiston	Rock & Roll
19	Soaring	Bobby Brewster Band	Jazz
20	Adventure	Dan Hogan	Rhythm & Blues
21	Crazy About You	Jake Foster	Country
22	Jumper	The Rockers	Rock & Roll
23	Breaking Up	Billy Bob	Country

Create an Employee Average Age Spreadsheet

New Skills: Using the Average Formula • Shading Cells • Creating a Custom Header

TASK AND PURPOSE:

Create a spreadsheet that shows the average age of the employees of Skateboards, Inc.

OVERVIEW:

Randy Boardman observed that his employees are agile, energetic, and vibrant individuals and decided it would be interesting to know the average age of his employees. You will provide him with the answer by creating a spreadsheet using the average formula.

STRATEGIES AND TIPS TO CONSIDER:

1.   This is an internal database. Keep it simple. No graphics are necessary (unless you want to insert a birthday cake for the fun of it).

2.   Read through all instructions before proceeding with the project.

INSTRUCTIONS, INFORMATION, AND REQUIRED CONTENT:

1.   Using Microsoft Excel, create a new blank workbook.

2.   Save the document as **Project E-4 Employee Average Age** in your "Excel Projects" folder under your "Skateboards, Inc. Simulation" folder.

3.   Format the width of columns A and B to 25, and column C to 15.

4.   Key the data as it appears in **Figure E-4-1** into the spreadsheet. Unless otherwise noted, the font should be set to Arial 10 point.
Note: You will be entering a formula later in the cell labeled <Formula>.

5.   Change the font size of cells A1 – C1 to 12 point; also center align and bold the cells.

6.   Shade cells A1 – C1 using a 25% gray fill color.

7.   Enter a formula in cell C21 that will compute the average age of the employees (given in cells C2 – C20).
Hint: Use "=AVERAGE"

8.   Center align cells C2 – C21 and format them as numbers displaying 0 decimals.

9.   Right align and bold cell B21.

10.   Format cell C21 as bold.

11.   Create a custom header and key the text provided below as the header. Center align the header and set the font to Arial 14 point bold.

        Skateboards, Inc. Average Age of Employees

12.   View the header using Print Preview to ensure that it has been set up properly.

13.   Carefully proofread your work for accuracy and format.

14.   Resave the file.

15.   Set the Print Area to include all cells containing data in the spreadsheet.

16.   Print Preview and adjust the Page Setup so that the spreadsheet fits on one page.

17.   Print a copy of the document if required by your instructor.

Figure E-4-1

	A	B	C
1	Employee Name	Title	Age
2	D.J. Jazz	Disc Jockey	25
3	Carl Pickering	Food Court Clerk	16
4	Christopher Edwards	Food Court Clerk	17
5	John Barnes	Food Court Clerk	18
6	Joshua Jones	General Manager	29
7	Katie Carrington	Housekeeper	23
8	Katelyn Nolin	Instructor	24
9	Artie Martin	Technician	28
10	Amy Reeve	Marketing	19
11	Christine Stone	Marketing	23
12	Rebecca Langford	Marketing Director	24
13	Annie Sheehan	Office Manager	21
14	Randy Boardman	President	36
15	Jennifer Burton	Pro Shop Clerk	19
16	Samantha Walters	Pro Shop Clerk	19
17	Kyle Logan	Pro Shop Manager	32
18	Alexander Butler	Security Guard	24
19	Antonio Reis	Security Guard	27
20	Doug Stanton	Technician	23
21		Average Age	<Formula>

Create a Projected Revenue Spreadsheet

New Skills: Using the Division (/) Operation in a Formula • Formatting Cells with Text Wrap • Formatting Cells as Percentage

TASK AND PURPOSE:

Create a spreadsheet for Skateboards, Inc. that will project the first month's arcade games revenue by game category (pinball machines, video games, sports table games, etc.). The report will also display the percentage of total revenue that each game category will generate.

OVERVIEW:

The Arcade at Skateboards, Inc. houses pinball machines, video games, sports table games, and other fun activities such as a photo booth, Skee-Ball Alley, and pool tables. Once the park opens for business, management will periodically need to assess the Arcade's revenue. A revenue projection for the first month of operation, broken down by game and category, is depicted in Figure E-5-1. At the end of each month, management will compare the projected revenue to the actual revenue received and make decisions regarding the replacement of games that are not producing sufficient revenue.

STRATEGIES AND TIPS TO CONSIDER:

1.   Use proper accounting style in formatting the spreadsheet.

2.   Carefully check your results after entering the formulas in the spreadsheet.

3.   Read through all instructions before proceeding with the project.

INSTRUCTIONS, INFORMATION, AND REQUIRED CONTENT:

1.   Using Microsoft Excel, create a new blank workbook.

2.   Save the document as **Project E-5 Projected Revenue Spreadsheet** in your "Excel Projects" folder under your "Skateboards, Inc. Simulation" folder.

3.   Format the width of column A to 25 and columns B – D to 10.

4.   Format cells A1 – D1 to bold, center align, and to wrap text. Also shade these cells using a 25% gray fill color.

5.   Key the data as it appears in **Figure E-5-1** into the spreadsheet. Unless otherwise noted, the font should be set to Arial 10 point.
     Note: You will be entering formulas later in the cells labeled <Formula>.

6.   Format cells A2, A9, A11, A18, A20, A24, A26, A30, and A32 to bold.

7.   Format cells B8, B17, B23, B29, C31, and D31 to display a bottom border.

8.   Format cells B3 – C32 to currency to display 2 decimals and the $ symbol.

9.   Format column D to percentage to display 2 decimals.

10.   Enter a formula in cell C9 that will sum the projected revenue for "Pinball Machines."
        Hint: Use the =SUM formula.

11.   Enter a formula in cell C18 that will sum the projected revenue for "Video Games."
        Hint: Use the =SUM formula.

12.   Enter a formula in cell C24 that will sum the projected revenue for "Sports Table Games."
        Hint: Use the =SUM formula.

13.   Enter a formula in cell C30 that will sum the projected revenue for the "Other Games" category.
        Hint: Use the =SUM formula.

14.   Enter a formula in cell C32 to sum the totals in cells C9, C18, C24, and C30.

15.   Enter a formula in cell D9 to compute "% of Total Projected Revenue" for the Pinball Machines. This is computed by dividing the "Total Pinball Machines" by the "Total Projected Game Revenue."
        Hint: C9/C32.

16.   Enter a formula in cell D18 to compute "% of Total Projected Revenue" for the Video Games. This is computed by dividing the "Total Video Games" by the "Total Projected Game Revenue."
        Hint: C18/C32.

17.   Enter a formula in cell D24 to compute "% of Total Projected Revenue" for the Sports Table Games. This is computed by dividing the "Total Sports Table Games" by the "Total Projected Game Revenue."
        Hint: C24/C32.

18.   Enter a formula in cell D30 to compute "% of Total Projected Revenue" for the Other Games category. This is computed by dividing the "Total Other Games" by the "Total Projected Game Revenue."
        Hint: C30/C32.

19.   Enter a formula in cell D32 to compute the sum of "% of Total Projected Revenue" column.
        Hint: Your answer should equal 100%.

20.   Bold cells C32 and D32.

21.   Create a custom header and key the text provided below as the header. Center align the header and set the font to Arial 14 point bold (insert the current month and year where indicated.)

Skateboards, Inc.
Arcade Games Projected Revenue
For Month of [insert current month], [insert current year]

22.   View the header using Print Preview to ensure that it has been set up properly.

23.   Carefully proofread your work for accuracy and format.

24.   Resave the file.

25.   Set the Print Area to include all cells containing data in the spreadsheet.

26.   Print Preview and adjust the Page Setup so that the spreadsheet fits on one page.

27.   Print a copy of the document if required by your instructor.

Figure E-5-1

	A	B	C	D
1	Category/Game	Projected Revenue	Projected Revenue by Game Category	% of Total Projected Revenue
2	Pinball Machines:			
3	Olympic Ski Racer	789.25		
4	Monsters from the Deep	850.5		
5	Speed-Racer	857.75		
6	Star-Blaster!	350		
7	Martians & Moonmen	380		
8	Truckin'			
9	Total Pinball Machines	717.25	<Formula>	<Formula>
10				
11	Video Games:			
12	Money Chase!	420		
13	Arachnids	287.5		
14	Bowl-away	625		
15	Zoom!	526		
16	Tornado Alley	380.5		
17	War Zone	467		
18	Total Video Games		<Formula>	<Formula>
19				
20	Sports Table Games:			
21	Foosball	675		
22	Football	408		
23	Soccer	623		
24	Total Sports Table Games		<Formula>	<Formula>
25				
26	Other Games:			
27	Photo Booth	790		
28	Skee-Ball Alley	127		
29	Pool Table	837		
30	Total Other Games		<Formula>	<Formula>
31				
32	Total Projected Game Revenue		<Formula>	<Formula>

Create a Pro Shop Equipment Inventory Report

New Skills: Using the Multiplication (*) Operation in a Formula • Using the AutoFill Feature

TASK AND PURPOSE:

Create a spreadsheet that lists the equipment for sale and inventory on hand in the Skateboards, Inc. Pro Shop. The list will assist the Pro Shop manager and staff members to answer customer inquiries about prices and product lines, help them to know when it is time to reorder products, and provide Skateboards, Inc.'s accountant with the value of the inventory.

OVERVIEW:

In order to stay organized and have the capacity to retrieve data quickly, businesses use spreadsheets to store various types of information. In this task, you will create a spreadsheet that shows the inventory of equipment for sale in the Skateboards, Inc. Pro Shop including the item description, vendor name, quantity sold, balance in inventory, and value of inventory.

STRATEGIES AND TIPS TO CONSIDER:

1. For this project, set the "Zoom" on the standard toolbar to 75% so that all of your columns are visible on the screen.

2. To format the cells in multiple columns simultaneously (when the columns to be formatted are not side-by-side), select all of the columns to be formatted by pointing your mouse to the letter at the top of the first column, left-click the mouse to select that column; then, while holding down the "control" key, click on the letter at the top of each of the other columns to be formatted.

3. When finished, use a calculator to spot-check the results of the formulas for accuracy.

4. Read through all instructions before proceeding with the project.

INSTRUCTIONS, INFORMATION, AND REQUIRED CONTENT:

1. Using Microsoft Excel, create a new blank workbook.

2. Save the document as **Project E-6 Pro Shop Equipment Inventory Report** in your "Excel Projects" folder under your "Skateboards, Inc. Simulation" folder.

3. Format the width of columns A, C, E, G, and I to 9, columns F and H to 11, B to 38, and D to 19.

4. Format the height of row 1 to 55.

5. Format cells A1 – I1 to bold, center align, and to wrap text. Also shade these cells using a 25% gray fill color.

6. Key the data as it appears in **Figure E-6-1** into the spreadsheet. Unless otherwise noted, the font should be set to Arial 10 point.
   Note: You will be entering formulas later in the cells labeled <Formula>.

7. Center align cells A2 – A22, C2 – C22, and F2 – H23.

8. Format cells E2 – E22 and I2 – I23 to currency to display 2 decimals and the $ symbol.

9. Enter a formula in cell H2 to compute the "# of Units in Inventory at End of Month" for the first item (Momentum Wrist Guards). This is computed by subtracting the "# of Units Sold" from the "# of Units in Inventory at Beginning of Month."
   Hint: Your answer should equal 15.

10. Use the AutoFill feature to copy the formula down column H to cell H22.

11. Enter a formula in cell I2 to compute the "Value of Inventory at End of Month" for the first item (Momentum Wrist Guards). This is computed by multiplying the "Price" by the "# of Units in Inventory at End of Month."
    Hint: Your answer should equal $269.85.

12. Use the AutoFill feature to copy the formula down column I to cell I22.

13. Enter a formula in cell F23 that totals the "# of Units in Inventory at Beginning of Month" column.
    Hint: Use =SUM.

14. Use the AutoFill feature to copy the formulas to cells G23 – I23 to compute the remaining column sum totals.

15. Bold row 23.

16. Create a custom header and key the text provided below as the header. Center align the header and set the font to Arial, 10 point, bold (insert the current month and year where indicated.)

    Skateboards, Inc.
    Pro-Shop Equipment Inventory Report
    [insert current month] , 20__

17. View the header using Print Preview to ensure that it has been set up properly.

18. Carefully proofread your work for accuracy and format.

19. Resave the file.

20. Set the Print Area to include all cells containing data in the spreadsheet.

21. Print Preview and adjust the Page Setup so that the spreadsheet fits on one page.

22. Print a copy of the document if required by your instructor.

Figure E-6-1

	A	B	C	D	E	F	G	H	I
	Item #	Item Description	Size	Vendor Name	Price	# of Units in Inventory at Beginning of Month	# of Units Sold	# of Units in Inventory at End of Month	Value of Inventory at End of Month
1									
2	S1272	Momentum Wrist Guards	S,M,L	Momentum, Inc.	17.99	22	7	<Formula>	<Formula>
3	S2182	Momentum Knee Pads	S,M,L	Momentum, Inc.	42.99	17	9	<Formula>	<Formula>
4	S3331	Momentum Elbow Guards	S,M,L	Momentum, Inc.	21.99	21	15	<Formula>	<Formula>
5	S3791	Momentum Combo Pack	S,M,L	Momentum, Inc.	49.99	35	32	<Formula>	<Formula>
6	S4295	Multi-purpose Skate Pack	N/A	Momentum, Inc.	31.95	37	7	<Formula>	<Formula>
7	S5100	T-shirt/Skateboards Inc. Logo	S,M,L,XL	Wheeling Clothing Co.	9.99	50	22	<Formula>	<Formula>
8	S5221	Skateboards Inc. Baseball Cap	S,M,L	Sport Caps Company	8.99	50	28	<Formula>	<Formula>
9	S7134	Pro-Tech Ace Helmet	S,M,L	Pro-Tech Supply	34.99	29	17	<Formula>	<Formula>
10	S7142	Helmet Liners	N/A	Pro-Tech Supply	11.49	47	38	<Formula>	<Formula>
11	S8201	Riser Pads (2-pack)	N/A	Flying Boards, Inc.	2.99	50	40	<Formula>	<Formula>
12	S1872	Grip Tape	N/A	Flying Boards, Inc.	5.99	75	52	<Formula>	<Formula>
13	S9235	High-speed Bearings	N/A	Velocity, Inc.	18.99	100	21	<Formula>	<Formula>
14	S9281	Consolidated Filter AB5 Bearings	N/A	Velocity, Inc.	15.99	77	11	<Formula>	<Formula>
15	S5316	Topspeed 51mm Wheels (1 wheel per pkg.)	N/A	Topspeed Enterprises	4.99	210	80	<Formula>	<Formula>
16	S5422	Speed Demon 53mm Wheels	N/A	Speed Demon	3.99	78	23	<Formula>	<Formula>
17	S6390	Topspeed Mercenary Logo Board	N/A	Topspeed Enterprises	39.99	32	11	<Formula>	<Formula>
18	S7000	Consolidated Hardware Packet	N/A	Topspeed Enterprises	7	7	5	<Formula>	<Formula>
19	I2896	Inline Skates	6-12	Decker Industries	69.99	32	12	<Formula>	<Formula>
20	S5023	Skateboarding for Beginners Book	N/A	Ace Book Company	14.99	29	21	<Formula>	<Formula>
21	S2145	Skateboards, Inc. Decals (3 per pkg.)	N/A	Custom Decals Co.	0.99	88	76	<Formula>	<Formula>
22	S2146	Skateboards, Inc. Logo Stickers (3 per pkg.)	N/A	Custom Decals Co.	0.49	130	59	<Formula>	<Formula>
23		TOTALS			<Formula>	<Formula>	<Formula>	<Formula>	<Formula>

SKATEBOARDS, INC.

PART 3:
ACCESS

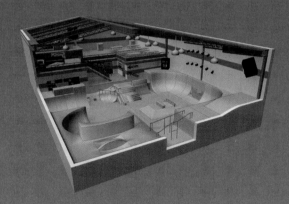

PROJECTS INCLUDED:

Project A-1:*   Create an Employee Database
Project A-2:   Create a Member Database
Project A-3:   Create an Advertiser Database

*This project must be completed before beginning Microsoft Word *Project W-10: Employee Welcome Letter*.

Approx. Completion Time: .75 hrs.

Create an Employee Database

New Skills: Entering Field Names • Defining Field Data Types • Defining Field Size • Entering Data into a Database • Using Design View

! **IMPORTANT NOTE: This project must be completed prior to beginning "Project W-10: Create an Employee Welcome Letter Mail Merge" in the Microsoft Word section of this book.**

TASK AND PURPOSE:

Create an employee database for Skateboards, Inc. that includes employee contact information (name, home address, telephone number), position title, location within the park, and extension number. This database will be used to generate a directory of employee names, work locations, and extension numbers to be distributed to all employees of the park. It will also be useful in creating mail-merge documents to employees including letters or memorandums, envelopes, and labels.

OVERVIEW:

Because businesses communicate frequently with their employees for numerous reasons, it is extremely important that they maintain an up-to-date list of current employee data. Employee databases can be very complex or very basic. In this project, you will create a very basic employee database.

STRATEGIES AND TIPS TO CONSIDER:

1. Do not use spaces between words in database field names.

2. Be consistent in the wording of the data that you enter in the table so that the results are accurate when you query the table.

3. A Microsoft Access tip: always close all open screens, one by one, before finally closing the Access program.

4. Read through all instructions before proceeding with the project.

INSTRUCTIONS, INFORMATION, AND REQUIRED CONTENT:

1. Using Microsoft Access, open a new blank database.

2. Save the document as **Project A-1 Employee Database** in your "Access Projects" folder under your "Skateboards, Inc. Simulation" folder.

3. Create a new Table using the Design View mode.

4. Define the structure of the database Table by entering the following Field Names, Data Types, Descriptions, and Field Sizes provided in **Figure A-1-1** below.
Note: Do not use spaces when entering field names.

Figure A-1-1

Field Name	Data Type	Description	Field Size
Salutation	Text	Salutation	3
Lname	Text	Last Name	50
Fname	Text	First Name	50
Street	Text	Street Address	25
City	Text	City	25
State	Text	State	2
Zip	Text	Zip Code	5
Tel	Text	Telephone Number	12
Title	Text	Position Title	50
Location	Text	Location/Department	50
TelExt	Text	Telephone Extension	3

5. Close the Table Design View window. When prompted to save the design of the table, save it as **Employee Information**. Do not define a Primary Key for this table.

6. Open the "Employee Information" table and key the information for each employee record provided in **Figure A-1-2** into the table.
Note: The record numbers are provided for reference purposes only and should not be entered in the table.

7. Carefully proofread your work for accuracy and format.

8. Close the table. If prompted to save the table, click "Yes."

9. Print Preview and adjust the Page Setup so the document fits on one page.

10. Print a copy of the "Employee Information" table if required by your instructor.

Figure A-1-2

Record #	Salutation	Lname	Fname	Street	City	State	Zip	Tel	Title	Location	TelExt
1	Mr.	Barnes	John	33 Wellington Blvd.	Rapid City	SD	57703	605-839-0815	Food Court Clerk	Food Court	213
2	Mr.	Boardman	Randy	360 Jackson Blvd.	Rapid City	SD	57702	888-555-7245	President	General Office	211
3	Ms.	Burton	Jennifer	52 Meadow Lane	Midland	SD	57552	605-310-8811	Pro Shop Clerk	Pro Shop	212
4	Mr.	Butler	Alexander	100 Nelson Road	Sioux Falls	SD	57107	605-735-1096	Security Guard	Security Office	214
5	Ms.	Carrington	Katie	97 Bay Street	Edgemont	SD	57735	605-495-0913	Housekeeper	Facilities Room	215
6	Mr.	Edwards	Christopher	49 Grand Avenue	Springfield	SD	57062	605-938-3553	Food Court Clerk	Food Court	221
7	Mr.	Jazz	D.J.	3053 Center Street	Rapid City	SD	57703	605-873-3212	Disc Jockey	Music Booth	222
8	Mr.	Jones	Joshua	203 Water Street	Clear Lake	SD	57226	605-353-2233	General Manager	General Office	226
9	Ms.	Langford	Rebecca	94 Laurel Lane	Wagner	SD	57361	605-767-8888	Marketing Director	General Office	227
10	Mr.	Logan	Kyle	21 Cottonwood Road	Brookings	SD	57006	605-421-6533	Pro Shop Manager	Pro Shop	217
11	Mr.	Martin	Artie	2 Lexington Road	Midland	SD	57552	605-310-6432	Technician	Facilities Room	216
12	Ms.	Nolin	Katelyn	21 Riverside Drive	Springfield	SD	57062	605-943-5455	Instructor	General Office	218
13	Mr.	Pickering	Carl	355 Greenbrier Street	Sioux Falls	SD	57107	605-755-3035	Food Court Clerk	Food Court	219
14	Ms.	Reeve	Amy	72 Ledge Street	Edgemont	SD	57735	605-493-5395	Marketing Associate	General Office	220
15	Mr.	Reis	Antonio	159 Anderson Way	Wagner	SD	57361	605-767-5349	Security Guard	Security Office	228
16	Ms.	Sheehan	Annie	76 Middle Road	Midland	SD	57552	605-313-5322	Office Manager	General Office	229
17	Mr.	Stanton	Doug	31 Maple Street	Rapid City	SD	57703	605-861-0395	Technician	Pro Shop	223
18	Ms.	Stone	Christine	182 Main Street	Rapid City	SD	57703	605-844-8396	Marketing Associate	General Office	225
19	Ms.	Walters	Samantha	18 Cove Street	Edgemont	SD	57735	605-499-3912	Pro Shop Clerk	Pro Shop	224

SKATEBOARDS, INC.

Create a Member Database

New Skills: Creating Forms • Designing/Customizing Forms • Using Queries

TASK AND PURPOSE:

Create a database listing the name, address, telephone number, and birth date of the members who have already joined Skateboards, Inc. The information in this database will be used to contact members about upcoming events, contests, promotions, and other matters pertaining to membership. The database will be updated continually as new members join Skateboards, Inc.

OVERVIEW:

Recreational facilities often create promotions and contests to help generate an increase in membership. One promotion that is particularly exciting at Skateboards, Inc. is that members will be invited to bring a friend to skate for free as a guest of the park on the member's birthday. General Manager Joshua Jones asks you to do three things: 1) create a member database 2) create a form listing the name and birth date of each member, and 3) create a query listing the names and addresses of members who live in Rapid City.

STRATEGIES AND TIPS TO CONSIDER:

1.   Do not use spaces between words in database field names.

2.   Be consistent in the wording of the data that you enter in the table so that the results are accurate when you query the table.

3.   A Microsoft Access tip: always close all open screens, one by one, before finally closing the Access program.

4.   Have fun designing the form. Though not required, you might want to experiment with using color for either individual fields or the background of the form.

5.   Read through all instructions before proceeding with the project.

INSTRUCTIONS, INFORMATION, AND REQUIRED CONTENT:

1.   Using Microsoft Access, open a new blank database.

2.   Save the document as **Project A-2 Member Database** in your "Access Projects" folder under your "Skateboards, Inc. Simulation" folder.

3.   Create a new Table using the Design View mode.

4. Define the structure of the database Table by entering the following Field Names, Data Types, Descriptions, and Field Sizes provided in **Figure A-2-1** below.
Note: Do not use spaces when entering field names.

Figure A-2-1

Field Name	Data Type	Description	Field Size
LastName	Text	Member's Last Name	25
FirstName	Text	Member's First Name	25
Address	Text	Member's Street Address	30
City	Text	Member's City	25
State	Text	Member's State	2
Zip	Text	Member's Zip Code	5
Telephone	Text	Member's Telephone Number	12
* BirthDate	Date/Time	Member's Birth Date	N/A (See below)

*Format the BirthDate field Data Type as Date/Time and choose the Short Date option.
Example: 6/19/1990

5. Close the Table Design view window. When prompted to save the design of the table, save it as **Member Information**. Do not define a Primary Key for this table.

6. Open the "Member Information" table and key the information for each member record provided in **Figure A-2-2** into the table.
Note: The record numbers are provided for reference purposes only and should not be entered in the table.

7. Close the table. If prompted to save the table, click "Yes."

8. Click on Forms and create a form that lists each member's last name, first name, and birth date. Use your own creativity to create an attractive format for the form.

9. Close the form. When prompted to save the design of the form, save it as **Member Birth Dates.**

10. Click on Query and, using the Member Information table, create a query that lists the last name, first name, and telephone number of all members who live in Rapid City.
Hint: In this query, the criteria should be equal to "Rapid City" in the City field.

11. Close the Query. When prompted to save the design of the query, save it as **Members from Rapid City.**

12. Carefully proofread your work for accuracy and format.

13. Print a copy of the table, the form, and the query if required by your instructor. Adjust the Page Setup so that each document fits on one page.

Figure A-2-2

Record #	LastName	FirstName	Address	City	State	Zip	Telephone	BirthDate
1	Beaumont	Brian	118 Tickle Road	Rapid City	SD	57703	605-839-3939	2/28/1991
2	Brown	Denzel	13 Captain's Lane	Springfield	SD	57062	605-938-1923	12/19/1993
3	Burke	Thomas	38 Chippaway Road	Edgemont	SD	57735	605-495-3494	1/3/1983
4	Goodrow	Paul	108 Ruggles Road	Clear Lake	SD	57226	605-353-3444	3/10/1990
5	Hernandez	Jorge	1 Leeward Way	Wagner	SD	57361	605-767-4429	4/18/1987
6	Langley	Heather	791 Hathaway Road	Rapid City	SD	57703	605-899-5335	8/15/1992
7	Nolan	Nate	35 Catherine Road	Rapid City	SD	57703	605-739-8998	11/1/1989
8	Norwalk	Vic	57 Cedar Street	Sioux Falls	SD	57107	605-944-3614	4/19/1984
9	Spillane	Matt	383 David Street	Rapid City	SD	57703	605-888-3122	3/12/1988
10	Stetson	Jake	923 James Road	Midland	SD	57552	605-313-1237	4/17/1992
11	Stone	Shania	93 Oak Street	Rapid City	SD	57703	605-876-5243	7/13/1985
12	Striker	Joey	37 Webster Lane	Clear Lake	SD	57226	605-354-6622	2/14/1986
13	Walker	Duke	98 Dana Road	Rapid City	SD	57703	605-789-4439	12/31/1982
14	Ward	Jane	5979 Prince Highway	Midland	SD	57553	605-310-8832	9/27/1988

Create an Advertiser Database

New Skills: Creating a Report • Sorting Records

TASK AND PURPOSE:

Create a database listing the business name, contact person, address, telephone number, fax number, and email information of the local businesses participating in the banner advertising campaign for Skateboards, Inc. Office Manager Annie Sheehan will use the information in the database to prepare monthly invoices for the advertisers. Marketing Director Rebecca Langford will use it to communicate with advertisers about the campaign.

OVERVIEW:

Developed by Rebecca Langford, the campaign gives local business owners the opportunity to advertise their businesses on the big screen TVs and on banners of various sizes and colors that will hang from the rafters or be displayed on side walls at the park. Ms. Langford needs to contact the eleven advertisers, who have already enrolled, to remind them to submit the text and graphic information for their banner as soon as possible. This must be done so that Canvas Creations, the banner manufacturer, will have sufficient time to produce the banners prior to the Grand Opening. She asks you to create a report that lists the business name, contact person, phone number, and the contact person's email address.

STRATEGIES AND TIPS TO CONSIDER:

1. Do not use spaces between words in database field names.

2. Be consistent in the wording of the data that you enter in the table so that the results are accurate when you query the table.

3. A Microsoft Access tip: always close all open screens, one by one, before finally closing the Access program.

4. Read through all instructions before proceeding with the project.

INSTRUCTIONS, INFORMATION, AND REQUIRED CONTENT:

1. Using Microsoft Access, open a new blank database.

2. Save the document as **Project A-3 Advertiser Database** in your "Access Projects" folder under your "Skateboards, Inc. Simulation" folder.

3. Create a new Table using the Design View mode.

4. Define the structure of the database Table by entering the following Field Names, Data Types, Descriptions, and Field Sizes provided in **Figure A-3-1** below.
Note: Do not use spaces when entering field names.

Figure A-3-1

Field Name	Data Type	Description	Field Size
BusinessName	Text	Advertiser's Company Name	30
ContactPerson	Text	Advertiser's Contact Person	30
PhoneNumber	Text	Advertiser's Phone Number	12
FaxNumber	Text	Advertiser's Fax Number	12
Address	Text	Advertiser's Street Address	30
City	Text	Advertiser's City	30
State	Text	Advertiser's State	2
Zip	Text	Advertiser's Zip Code	5
ContactE-mail	Text	Advertiser's E-mail Address	50

5. Close the table design view window. When prompted to save the design of the table, save it as **Advertiser Information.** Do not define a Primary Key for this table.

6. Open the "Advertiser Information" table and key the information for each advertiser record provided in **Figure A-3-2** into the table.
Note: The record numbers are provided for reference purposes only and should not be entered in the table.

7. Close the table. If prompted to save the table, click "Yes."

8. Click on Reports and create a report that lists the business name, contact person, phone number, and the contact person's email address in ascending alphabetical order by business name. This report will be used to contact the eleven advertisers who have enrolled in the Skateboards, Inc. banner advertising campaign. Use your best judgment in formatting the look of the report.

9. Close the report. When prompted to save the design of the report, save it as **Advertiser Information Report.**

10. Carefully proofread your work for accuracy and format.

11. Print a copy of the table and the report if required by your instructor. Adjust the Page Setup so that each document fits on one page.

Figure A-3-2

Record #	BusinessName	ContactPerson	PhoneNumber	FaxNumber	Address	City	State	Zip	ContactE-mail
1	Aberdeen Workout Club	Diana Tara	605-305-3333	605-315-0393	1059 Second Ave.	Aberdeen	SD	57401	dtara@aberdeen.com
2	Ace Bookstore	Murray Ruben	605-325-3298	605-324-2009	154 Water Street	Watertown	SD	57735	mruben@ace.com
3	Clear Lake Electronics	Melinda Prada	605-317-7196	605-477-4400	2 Tyler Road	Clear Lake	SD	57226	mprada@clearlake.com
4	Mt. Rushmore Games	Clay Patterson	605-382-3855	605-382-2221	12 Middle Road	Rapid City	SD	57703	cpatterson@mtr.com
5	Northern Electronics	Robert Gifford	605-333-2300	605-334-0909	104 State Street	Watertown	SD	57735	rgifford@northern.com
6	Rapid City Motors	Guy Barlow	605-335-4403	605-333-9349	5 Beacon Way	Rapid City	SD	57703	gbarlow@rcmotors.com
7	Rapid City Pizza	Roberto Romo	605-325-6793	605-325-3232	32 Stokes Blvd.	Rapid City	SD	57703	rromo@rcpizza.com
8	Rapid City Sport Shop	Don Watkins	605-233-9230	605-237-4950	780 Broadway	Rapid City	SD	57703	dwatkins@rcsport.com
9	Salomon Clothing	Mark Bodek	605-373-0931	605-372-3232	12 Hoxey Road	Rapid City	SD	57703	mbodek@salomon.com
10	Speed Demon	Tyler Martin	605-444-2688	605-347-1279	402 Alley Road	Aberdeen	SD	57401	tmartin@sd.com
11	Wind Cave Music	Paul Zabak	605-239-9250	605-237-1235	3892 Ford Hwy.	Rapid City	SD	57703	pzabak@windcave.com

SKATEBOARDS, INC.

PART 4:
PUBLISHER

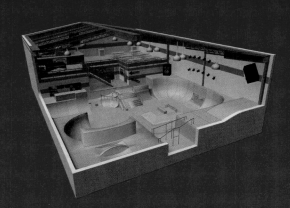

PROJECTS INCLUDED:

Note: The projects in this section can be completed using any desktop publishing software application.

*These projects are optional and are included as extra credit.

Create and Design a Business Card

New Skills: Creating and Designing a Business Card • Using the Rectangle Tool
• Using the Text Tool • Inserting Graphic Images

TASK AND PURPOSE:

Create and design a business card for Randy Boardman, President of Skateboards, Inc.

OVERVIEW:

A business card is a small, yet productive way to represent a person and their business. It includes a person's name, business affiliation, job title, address, telephone number, e-mail address, fax number, and Web address. This means that one tiny card can be the reason why people remember a person and their business. A business card is the handshake you leave behind after meeting someone.

STRATEGIES AND TIPS TO CONSIDER:

1. Since the business card does not offer much room, its design needs to be carefully planned.

2. A business card should encourage clients to remember a business in a favorable way. It exists for the purpose of making a business look good…not just good, but better than all of its competitors.

3. A business card should give potential clients a reason to keep it. You don't get business from a business card unless the person you give it to keeps it long enough to either call or visit your establishment.

4. A business card should stand out from competitors' cards so that it gets noticed.

5. The overall look and feel of a business card should match the type of business for which it is being designed. After the logo, your client's name should be the largest piece of information on the card.

6. Obtain some samples of real business cards and analyze them to help you design your own.

7. Plan the layout and design of your business card on paper first.

8. Read through all instructions before proceeding with the project.

INSTRUCTIONS, INFORMATION, AND REQUIRED CONTENT:

1. Before continuing, note that the layout, design, and fonts for this project will be left for you to decide.

2. Using Microsoft Publisher, or an equivalent desktop publishing software, create a new document.

3. Save the document as **Project P-1 Business Card** in your "Publisher Projects" folder under your "Skateboards, Inc. Simulation" folder.

4. Set the page size to 8.5 inches wide x 11 inches tall with .5 inch margins on all sides.

5. Using the rectangle tool, create a box that is 3.5 inches wide x 2 inches tall with a 1 point border. Place this box in the center of the page as shown in **Figure P-1-1**. The contents of the business card will be placed within this box.

Figure P-1-1

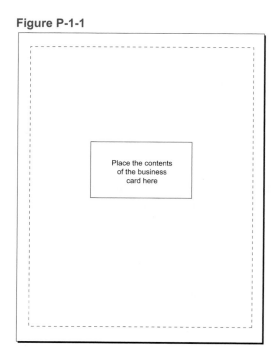

6. Insert the Skateboards, Inc. logo, installed from the Skateboards, Inc. Resource CD, on the business card. Resize the logo so it is in proportion with the rest of your document.

7.   Include the following information on the business card:

     Randy Boardman, President
     360 Jackson Boulevard, Rapid City, SD 57702
     Phone: 1-888-555-RAIL (7245)
     Fax: 1-888-555-PIPE (7473)
     Randy@skateboardsinc.net
     www.skateboardsinc.net

8.   Add additional text and/or graphic images that will help illustrate and enhance the look of the business card (optional).

9.   Carefully proofread your work for accuracy and format.

10. Resave the file.

11. Print a copy of the document if required by your instructor.

Create and Design an Employee Name Badge

New Skills: Creating and Designing a Name Badge • Using Color Fill
• Copying and Pasting Objects

TASK AND PURPOSE:

Create and design an employee name badge for all employees of Skateboards, Inc. Employees will wear their name badges at all times to identify them and their job title.

OVERVIEW:

An employee name badge can take on a variety of shapes and sizes and can be made out of many different materials. You will create a 3.5 inch wide x 2.5 inch tall name badge that all employees will wear to identify themselves to customers, vendors, and other employees of Skateboards, Inc. The name badge will also have a magnetic strip on the back (which acts like a key) to allow employees access to certain areas of the park marked "Employees Only." Employees will be provided with a lanyard to wear around their neck, and their name badge will be attached to it.

STRATEGIES AND TIPS TO CONSIDER:

1. Since the badge does not offer much room, its design needs to be carefully planned.

2. You will be creating two boxes for information on both the front and back of the name badge.

3. Consider using lines and borders to help create a balanced look and feel on your name badge.

4. Consider using some color to give your name badge a "stand out" effect.

5. Plan the layout and design of your employee name badge on paper first.

6. Read through all instructions before proceeding with the project.

INSTRUCTIONS, INFORMATION, AND REQUIRED CONTENT:

1. Before continuing, note that the layout, design, and fonts for this project will be left for you to decide.

2. Using Microsoft Publisher, or an equivalent desktop publishing software, create a new document.

3. Save the document as **Project P-2 Employee Name Badge** in your "Publisher Projects" folder under your "Skateboards, Inc. Simulation" folder.

4. Set the page size to 8.5 inches wide x 11 inches tall with .5 inch margins on all sides.

5. Using the rectangle tool, create two boxes that are 3.5 inches wide x 2.5 inches tall with a 1 point border and place them in the center of the page, one box above the other. The top box represents the front side of the name badge; the bottom box represents the back side of the name badge as shown in **Figure P-2-1**. The contents of the name badge will be placed within these boxes.

    Tip: Create one box, then use the copy and paste feature to create the second box.

Figure P-2-1

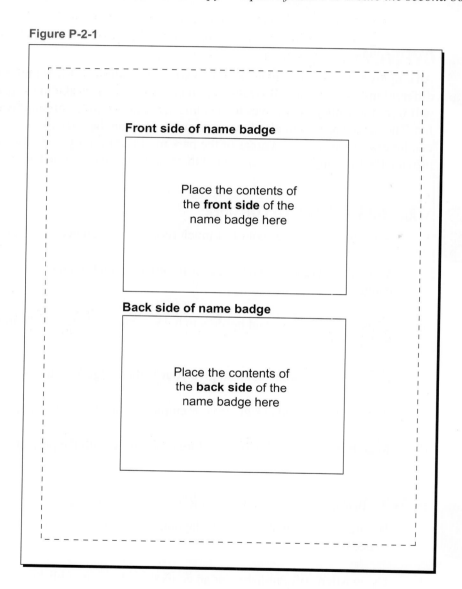

Front side of name badge

Place the contents of
the **front side** of the
name badge here

Back side of name badge

Place the contents of
the **back side** of the
name badge here

6.   Include the following on the **front side of the badge**:

- The Skateboards, Inc. logo installed from the Skateboards, Inc. Resource CD.
  Resize the logo so it is in proportion with the rest of your document.
- Your name, Microsoft Office Specialist

7.   Include the following on the **back side of the badge**:

- A rectangle box measuring 1 inch wide x 1.25 inches tall with a 1 point border. If you
  have access to a digital camera, insert your photo inside this border. If not, use a clipart
  image depicting a person's face.
- Using the rectangle tool, draw a box that measures 3.5 inches wide x .5 inches tall and
  place it .25 inches down from the top of the box. Fill the rectangle box with black (this is
  your magnetic strip for access into "Employees Only" areas of the park).
- The following disclaimer:

  This card is your official Skateboards, Inc. identification card and must be worn
  at all times when you are working at the park. It is the property of Skateboards,
  Inc. and must be surrendered upon request to administration or security. This card
  is nontransferable and may not be used by anyone other than you, the employee.
  Fraudulent or improper use is grounds for disciplinary action and/or dismissal. If
  this card is lost or stolen, contact the Skateboards, Inc. business office immediately.
  If found, return to: Skateboards, Inc., 360 Jackson Boulevard, Rapid City, SD
  57702.

8.   Add additional text and/or graphic images that will help illustrate and enhance the look of
       the front and back sides of the employee name badge (optional).

9.   Carefully proofread your work for accuracy and format.

10.   Resave the file.

11.   Print a copy of the document if required by your instructor.

Create and Design a Bumper Sticker

New Skills: Creating and Designing a Bumper Sticker

TASK AND PURPOSE:

Create and design a bumper sticker for Skateboards, Inc. to be used for promotional purposes. The bumper sticker will be given to customers.

OVERVIEW:

Bumper stickers are strips of adhesive paper of varying sizes with words, ideas or pictures printed on the non-adhesive side. They're meant to be placed on the bumper of your car but may be placed just about anywhere. With so many vehicles on the road today, they are a very useful marketing tool. Bumper stickers are also a useful way of showing support of an organization or business.

STRATEGIES AND TIPS TO CONSIDER:

1. To maximize visibility, use only one poster or block style font on the bumper sticker.

2. Limit the number of graphic images on the bumper sticker so it is not cluttered.

3. Plan the layout and design of your bumper sticker on paper first.

4. Read through all instructions before proceeding with the project.

INSTRUCTIONS, INFORMATION, AND REQUIRED CONTENT:

1. Before continuing, note that the layout, design, and fonts for this project will be left for you to decide.

2. Using Microsoft Publisher, or an equivalent desktop publishing software, create a new document.

3. Save the document as **Project P-3 Bumper Sticker** in your "Publisher Projects" folder under your "Skateboards, Inc. Simulation" folder.

4. Set the page size to 11 inches wide x 8.5 inches tall (landscape) with .25 inch margins on all sides.

5.   Using the rectangle tool, create a box that is 10 inches wide x 3 inches tall with a 1 point border. Place this box in the center of your document as shown in **Figure P-3-1**. Place the contents of the bumper sticker within this border.

Figure P-3-1

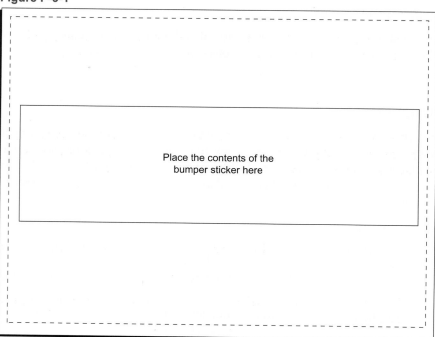

Place the contents of the
bumper sticker here

6.   Include the following on the bumper sticker:

 • The Skateboards, Inc. logo installed from the Skateboards, Inc. Resource CD.
   Resize the logo so it is in proportion with the rest of your document.
 • A large headline that reads: Rock and Roll at Skateboards, Inc.
 • The Skateboards, Inc. Web site address, which is: www.skateboardsinc.net

7.   Add additional text and/or graphic images that will help illustrate and enhance the look of the bumper sticker (optional).

8.   Carefully proofread your work for accuracy and format.

9.   Resave the file.

10.   Print a copy of the document if required by your instructor.

Create and Design a Grand Opening Advertisement

New Skills: Creating and Designing a Print Advertisement • Creating and Designing a Coupon

TASK AND PURPOSE:

Create and design a print advertisement for Skateboards, Inc. announcing the grand opening to the public. The advertisement will run in several local newspapers.

OVERVIEW:

Advertisements attract new customers, keep you in the competitive race, keep your business in people's minds, and give your business a successful image. Skateboards, Inc., being a brand new business, is attempting to spread the word of the grand opening.

STRATEGIES AND TIPS TO CONSIDER:

1. To create a professional-looking advertisement, use no more than three fonts in the advertisement.

2. Be careful of your font selection. Fonts that are too fancy or script-like can be hard to read and distracting.

3. One smart way to select the fonts for your headline to be noticed is to research fonts used by big corporations in their packaging, annual reports, magazine ads, etc. They spend thousands of dollars to have professional designers do their work.

4. Use starbursts and/or other call-out graphics to communicate important information.

5. Don't overcrowd your ad with too many graphic images as they will draw attention from the ad's message.

6. Plan the layout and design of your grand opening advertisement on paper first.

7. Read through all instructions before proceeding with the project.

INSTRUCTIONS, INFORMATION, AND REQUIRED CONTENT:

1. Before continuing, note that the layout, design, and fonts for this project will be left for you to decide.

2. Using Microsoft Publisher, or an equivalent desktop publishing software, create a new document.

3. Save the document as **Project P-4 Grand Opening Advertisement** in your "Publisher Projects" folder under your "Skateboards, Inc. Simulation" folder.

4. Set the page size to 8.5 inches wide x 11 inches tall with .5 inch margins on all sides.

5. Using the rectangle tool, create a box that is 6.5 inches wide x 8 inches tall with a 1 point border. Place this box in the center of your document as shown in **Figure P-4-1**. Place the contents of the advertisement within this border.

Figure P-4-1

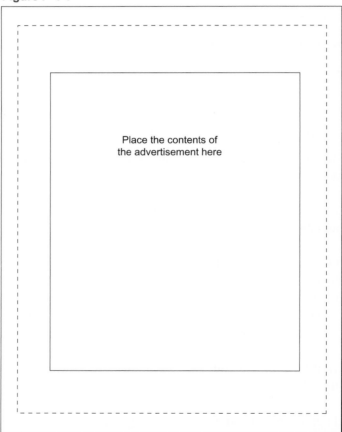

Place the contents of the advertisement here

6. Include an eye-catching headline in the advertisement that captures the attention of prospective readers. Place the headline at the top of your advertisement.

    Example: Grand Opening of Skateboards, Inc. or Attention Fellow Skateboarders

7. Include the following grand opening date and place it at the top of your advertisement where it can be easily seen:

    June 1, 20__

8. Include the Skateboards, Inc. logo in the advertisement installed from the Skateboards, Inc. Resource CD. Resize the logo so it is in proportion with the rest of your document.

9. Include the 3-D Sky View image of Skateboards, Inc. in the advertisement (installed from the Skateboards, Inc. Resource CD). Resize the image so it is in proportion with the rest of your document.

10. Include the following contact information in the advertisement:

    360 Jackson Boulevard, Rapid City, SD 57702
    Phone: 1-888-555-RAIL (7245)
    Fax: 1-888-555-PIPE (7473)
    info@skateboardsinc.net
    www.skateboardsinc.net

11. Include the following hours of operation and text in the advertisement:

    Monday-Friday   3 pm – 10 pm
    Saturday   9 am – 10 pm
    Sunday   9 am – 8 pm
    (Hours change during school vacations and summer – call 1-888-555-7245)

12. Include the following text and pro skateboarders' names who will be attending the grand opening event in the advertisement:

    Meet Pro Skateboarders Andy Caron and Amy MacDonald

13. Include the following headline and bullet list in a square or rectangular box.

    "ROCK AND ROLL INTO SKATEBOARDS, INC."
    • Ride our quarter pipes, ramps, and rails
    • Enjoy a Kickflip Burger at "The Skateboard Shack"
    • Play Skee-Ball or Tornado Alley in our Arcade
    • Browse through our new Pro Shop
    • Or, just hang out with your fellow skateboarders in our lounge and listen to D.J. Jazz play your favorite tunes

14. Create a cut-out style coupon (with a dashed border) that includes the following information:
    Tip: *Use a scissor graphic and place it on the dashed line.*

    • One day free trial when you present this coupon
    • In fine print, include text that reads "Offer expires on <insert date>"

15. Across the bottom of your ad in bold lettering include the following information:

     Everyone who skates at Skateboards, Inc. must have a signed waiver on file with us. No Exceptions!

16. Add additional text and/or graphic images that will help illustrate and enhance the look of the advertisement (optional).

17. Carefully proofread your work for accuracy and format.

18. Resave the file.

19. Print a copy of the document if required by your instructor.

Create and Design a Coupon Flyer

New Skills: Creating and Designing a Flyer

TASK AND PURPOSE:

To encourage potential customers to visit the establishment, Randy Boardman, President of Skateboards, Inc., would like you to create and design a coupon flyer. This flyer will be distributed at the grand opening and placed in the park and at various high-traffic spots throughout Rapid City, such as supermarkets, schools, and convenience stores.

OVERVIEW:

Sales promotions are important marketing tools in today's businesses. Coupons are the primary vehicle in sales promotions. Mr. Boardman is trying to attract attention to his new business. You will be designing a coupon flyer which is intended to draw in new clientele by offering different sales promotions.

STRATEGIES AND TIPS TO CONSIDER:

1. Use incentives to get people to act now.

2. When choosing graphics, it will be more effective to include one or two larger graphics than to clutter the page with numerous small graphics.

3. When creating your coupons, use a dotted-line border with a small graphic of scissors placed on one of the border sides to encourage customers to cut out and use the coupons.

4. Plan the layout and design of your coupon flyer on paper first.

5. Read through all instructions before proceeding with the project.

INSTRUCTIONS, INFORMATION, AND REQUIRED CONTENT:

1. Before continuing, note that the layout, design, and fonts for this project will be left for you to decide.

2. Using Microsoft Publisher, or an equivalent desktop publishing software, create a new document.

3. Save the document as **Project P-5 Coupon Flyer** in your "Publisher Projects" folder under your "Skateboards, Inc. Simulation" folder.

4. Set the page size to 8.5 inches wide x 11 inches tall with a .5 inch margin on all sides.

5. Using the rectangle tool, create a box that uses a 3 point border. Size the box so that it aligns with the page margins as shown in **Figure P-5-1**. Place the contents of the flyer within this border.

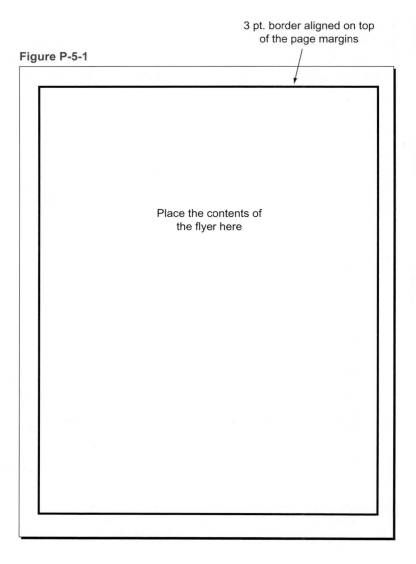

Figure P-5-1

3 pt. border aligned on top of the page margins

Place the contents of the flyer here

6. At the top of the flyer, include a simple, easy-to-read headline.

    Example: Skate Over to Skateboards, Inc.!

7. Insert the Skateboards, Inc. logo installed from the Skateboards, Inc. Resource CD. Resize the logo so it is in proportion with the rest of your document.

8. Include the following contact information on the flyer:

    360 Jackson Boulevard
    Rapid City, SD 57702
    Phone: 1-888-555-RAIL (7245)
    Fax: 1-888-555-PIPE (7473)
    info@skateboardsinc.net
    www.skateboardsinc.net

9. Include the following hours of operation and text on the flyer:

Monday-Friday	3 pm – 10 pm
Saturday	9 am – 10 pm
Sunday	9 am – 8 pm

    (Hours change during school vacations and summer – call 1-888-555-7245)

10. Include four cut-out style coupons on the flyer. Add one small graphic image to each coupon to enhance the look and appeal of each coupon.

Coupon #1:	Purchase a one-year membership and receive a FREE Skateboards, Inc. t-shirt from our pro shop.
Coupon #2:	$10 off a weekday one-hour skateboard or rollerblade lesson.
Coupon #3:	FREE beverage with any $5 purchase in our food court.
Coupon #4:	Spend $50 in our Pro Shop and receive 25 FREE tokens to our Arcade.

11. Add the following text in small print to the bottom of each coupon:

    Offer expires on July 15, 20__.
    Limit: One coupon per person.

12. Across the bottom of the flyer in bold lettering include the following text:

    Everyone who skates at Skateboards, Inc. must have a signed waiver on file with us. No Exceptions!

13. Add additional text and/or graphic images that will help illustrate and enhance the look and appeal of the flyer (optional).

14. Carefully proofread your work for accuracy and format.

15. Resave the file.

16. Print a copy of the document if required by your instructor.

Create and Design a Booklet-Style Food Menu

New Skills: Creating and Designing a Booklet Style Menu • Inserting Columns and Guides

TASK AND PURPOSE:

Create and design a booklet-style food menu for the Skateboards, Inc. food court called "The Skateboard Shack." The menu will be distributed throughout the park and will be displayed on the Web site.

OVERVIEW:

A menu is a list of food items offered by an establishment that serves food. The menu is not only going to be used for the paper version, but the inside of the menu will be the prototype for a large menu board that will be constructed and placed above the food court ("The Skateboard Shack").

STRATEGIES AND TIPS TO CONSIDER:

1. The menu will be designed using a booklet-style format printed on two sides. When folded in half the long way (landscape), the menu will be divided into four equal panels as shown in **Figure P-6-1**. Remember, the inside of the menu is being used as the prototype for the menu board above the food court.

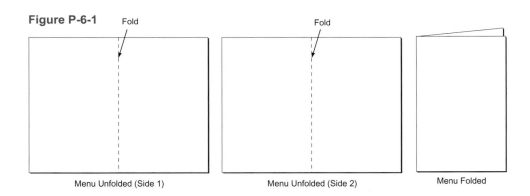

Figure P-6-1

Fold · Fold

Menu Unfolded (Side 1) · Menu Unfolded (Side 2) · Menu Folded

2. Highlight the most important menu items using bold face type.

3. Use at least two different fonts. One font for the menu items and their prices, and another for subtext that describes the menu items. Use fonts that are easy to read.

4. Keep the menu clean, uncluttered, and legible.

5. Use graphics throughout the menu to bring the food items to life.

6. Consider where you are placing menu items. Appetizers almost always go first.

7. Obtain some samples of menus by visiting establishments and doing some on-line research. Analyze them to come up with your own design.

8. Have fun with this project, adding your own design style to the menu. Create a menu that makes the consumer hungry for what is being offered.

9. Plan the layout and design of your menu on paper first.

10. Read through all instructions before proceeding with the project.

 ## INSTRUCTIONS, INFORMATION, AND REQUIRED CONTENT:

1. Before continuing, note that the layout, design, and fonts for this project will be left for you to decide.

2. Using Microsoft Publisher, or an equivalent desktop publishing software, create a new **two-page** document.

3. Save the document as **Project P-6 Menu** in your "Publisher Projects" folder under your "Skateboards, Inc. Simulation" folder.

4. Set the page size to 11 inches wide x 8.5 inches tall (landscape) with .30 inch margins on all sides.

5. On each page, insert two column guides with a .5 inch gutter (to allow room for folding the menu in half). The menu should now be divided into two panels on each page as shown in **Figure P-6-2**. Note how the panels are labeled on each side. The contents of the menu will be placed in its respective places according to the instructions that follow.

Figure P-6-2

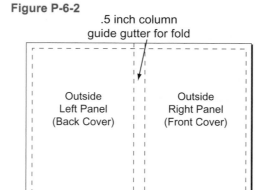
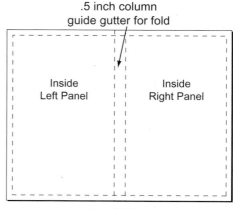

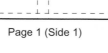

6. On the **Outside Right Panel** (front cover) of the menu, include the following:

    - The Skateboards, Inc. logo installed from the Skateboards, Inc. Resource CD.
      Resize the logo so it is in proportion with the rest of your document.
    - The text: "Welcome to The Skateboard Shack"
    - The text: "Rapid City's latest and greatest snack attack shack!"
    - Add additional text and/or graphic images that will help to enhance the look and
      appearance of the outside right panel.
    - Add a bordered frame around the information on the panel to give it a neat appearance.

7. On the **Outside Left Panel** (back cover) of the menu, include the following:

    - The text: "Skate by anytime. Thank you for your patronage."
    - The Skateboards, Inc. logo installed from the Skateboards, Inc. Resource CD.
      Resize the logo so it is in proportion with the rest of your document.
    - Include the following hours of operation and text:
      HOURS OF OPERATION:
      Monday - Friday   3 pm - 10 pm
      Saturday   9 am - 10 pm
      Sunday   9 am - 8 pm
      (Hours of operation follow park hours)
      Note: Grilled or fried menu items must be ordered 1/2 hour before closing!
    - Add additional text and/or graphic images that will help to enhance the look and
      appearance of the outside left panel.
    - Add a bordered frame around the information on the panel to give it a neat appearance.

8. On the **Inside Left and Right Panels** of the menu, add the Skateboard Shack's menu items
    and prices listed below:

Appetizers
Switch-Stance Snack Attack
Perfect for sharing. Combo with buffalo wings, nachos, onion rings
and chili cheese fries served with blue cheese or honey-mustard sauces for dipping. $6.95
Boardslide Buffalo Wings
Blazing, boneless crispy breaded wings served with blue cheese dressing. $5.95
Nollie Nachos
Crispy tortillas oozing with cheese $4.25
Super Nollie Nachos
Crispy tortillas loaded (oozing with cheese, refried beans, and nacho meat) $5.95
Ollie Onion Rings
Crispy onion rings ready to dip into any one of three sauces: ranch dressing, barbecue
sauce or honey mustard $4.95
Chili Cheese Fries
You're in for a real treat. Taste these crispy fries topped with warm cheddar cheese sauce,
crisp bacon and scallions served with ranch dressing for dipping $4.95

Burgers and Hot Dogs
Kickflip Burger (served with French Fries)
Our mouth-watering, juicy flame-broiled burger with lettuce, tomato, pickle and onion $5.95
Add cheese for .25 extra
Halfpipe Hot Dog (served with French Fries)
Our juicy foot-long hot dog cooked to perfection $4.95
With chili $5.25

"Grind"ers
Italian, Roast Beef, Tuna, Steak & Cheese, or Turkey Breast
All "Grind"ers are 6-inch subs and come with a snack size bag of potato chips. Add lettuce and tomato at no extra charge. $5.95

Pizzas
Skateboard Supreme
Cheese pizza with pepperoni, sausage, ham, meatball, onions, peppers, and mushrooms $9.95
360 Pizza
Whole cheese pizza with up to three toppings (pepperoni, sausage, ham, meatball, onions, peppers, or mushrooms) $8.95
180 Pizza
½ of a 360 with your choice of three toppings (pepperoni, sausage, ham, meatball, onions, peppers, or mushrooms) $6.95

Beverages
Coke, Sprite, Orange, Root Beer, Diet Coke, or Bottled Water $1.75

Desserts
Popcorn $1.75
Giant Pretzels (cinnamon & sugar or salt) $1.75
Brownies $1.25
Cookies (2) $1.25
Ice Cream Sandwich $1.75
Popsicle $1.25

9. Add additional text and/or graphic images that will help to enhance the look and appearance of the inside left and right panels.

10. Add a bordered frame around the information on the inside left and right panels to give the menu a neat appearance.

11. Carefully proofread your work for accuracy and format.

12. Resave the file.

13. Print a copy of the document if required by your instructor.
    Suggested: Print both sides of the menu on one page and fold in half.

Create and Design a Three-Panel Brochure (Extra Credit)

New Skills: Creating and Designing a Three-Panel Brochure

TASK AND PURPOSE:

Create and design a three-panel informational brochure for Skateboards, Inc. that will be located at the customer service desk, placed in membership packets, and displayed in various retail outlets throughout Rapid City.

OVERVIEW:

Brochures are a great way to package a lot of information about your business into a format that is easily mailed or handed out or given to current clients to pass on to possible referrals. Brochures usually have only a matter of seconds to capture someone's interest. Make sure yours has a readable, eye-catching design and focuses on what the patrons will receive rather than on what you do.

STRATEGIES AND TIPS TO CONSIDER:

1. The brochure will be designed using a three-panel, two-sided format. When folded in thirds the long way (landscape), the brochure will be divided into six equal panels (three on each side) as shown in **Figure P-7-1**.

Figure P-7-1

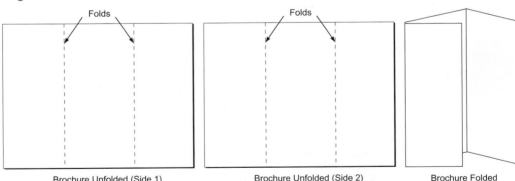

Brochure Unfolded (Side 1)   Brochure Unfolded (Side 2)   Brochure Folded

2. Good brochure design involves not simply producing a flashy design, but a careful analysis of your target market in order to make a great first impression.

3. When used correctly, brochures can position a company against its competitors, communicate the benefits of products or services, and motivate prospects to take action.

4. Your goal is to get potential patrons to see your brochure, be curious enough to pick it up and, even more important, keep it.

5.   Brochures should not be boring. If your brochure contains miles of text, no one is going to read through it. Make sure that you have filled the brochure with eye-catching graphics so that it is appealing and easy to read. Make sure that the headings are self-explanatory, so even if your brochure is not read in its entirety, its message is still delivered.

6.   The most obvious, yet often overlooked, piece of information on a brochure is the contact details. Your brochure should prominently display the Skateboards, Inc. logo, address, email address, phone numbers, and other vital information that customers can use to contact the establishment.

7.   Consider using a border on the inside three panels of the brochure to "frame" the information contained on them.

8.   When inserting separate pieces of information, consider inserting the information into separate text boxes. This will make it easier if you decide to move information around during the design process.

9.   To assist you in the layout and design of your brochure, fold a blank sheet of paper, holding it the long way (landscape), into three equal columns. Label these columns as indicated in the page setup instructions and illustrations for this section.

10.   Plan the layout and design of your brochure on paper first.

11.   Read through all instructions before proceeding with the project.

INSTRUCTIONS, INFORMATION, AND REQUIRED CONTENT:

1.   Before continuing, note that the layout, design, and fonts for this project will be left for you to decide.

2.   Using Microsoft Publisher, or an equivalent desktop publishing software, create a new **two-page** document.

3.   Save the document as **Project P-7 Three-Panel Brochure** in your "Publisher Projects" folder under your "Skateboards, Inc. Simulation" folder.

4.   Set the page size to 11 inches wide x 8.5 inches tall (landscape) with .30 inch margins on all sides.

5. On each page, insert three column guides with a .5 inch gutter (to allow room for folding the brochure in thirds). The brochure should now be divided into three panels on each page as shown in **Figure P-7-2**. Note how the panels are labeled on each side. The contents of the brochure will be placed according to the instructions that follow.

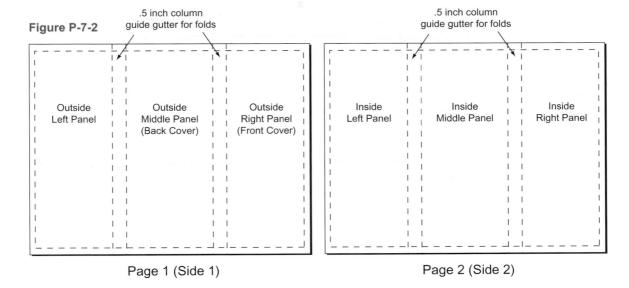

Figure P-7-2

.5 inch column guide gutter for folds

Outside Left Panel

Outside Middle Panel (Back Cover)

Outside Right Panel (Front Cover)

Page 1 (Side 1)

.5 inch column guide gutter for folds

Inside Left Panel

Inside Middle Panel

Inside Right Panel

Page 2 (Side 2)

6. On the **Outside Right Panel** (front cover) of the brochure, include the following:

    • The Skateboards, Inc. logo and 3-D Sky View image installed from the Skateboards, Inc. Resource CD. Resize the images so they are in proportion with the rest of your document.
    • Create an eye-catching headline that entices readers to open the brochure.
    Example: Rapid City's Latest and Greatest Indoor Skateboard/Rollerblade Park
    • Add additional text and/or graphic images that will encourage readers to continue reading the brochure.

7. On the **Outside Middle Panel** (back cover) of the brochure, include the following:

    • List the following employees of the park:
    John Barnes, Randy Boardman, Jennifer Burton, Alexander Butler, Katie Carrington, Christopher Edwards, Jay Johnson, Rebecca Langford, Kyle Logan, Artie Martin, Katelyn Nolin, Carl Pickering, Amy Reeve, Antonio Reis, Annie Sheehan, Doug Stanton, Christine Stone, and Samantha Walters

    • 360 Jackson Boulevard
    Rapid City, SD 57702
    Phone: 1-888-555-RAIL (7245)
    Fax: 1-888-555-PIPE (7473)
    info@skateboardsinc.net
    www.skateboardsinc.net

8.   Add additional text and/or graphic images that will help to enhance the look and appearance of the outside middle panel of the brochure.

9.   On the **Outside Left Panel** of the brochure, include the following features of the park:

- Skateboards, Inc., Rapid City's latest and greatest indoor skateboard and rollerblade park, opened its doors on June 1, 20__. With everything from fun boxes to quarter pipes and rails...we have it all.
- Skateboards, Inc. Pro Shop will definitely meet your every need in boards, rollerblades, wheels, parts, clothing, and much more.
- Stop by our Arcade and play one of the many new games including Zoom, Truckin', or Tornado Alley.
- Skateboards, Inc. is also the home of "The Skateboard Shack," Rapid City's latest and greatest snack attack shack. It features everything from Ollie Onion Rings, to our mouthwatering Kickflip Burger, to a Skateboard Supreme Pizza. You will absolutely "flip" over our desserts.
- Hang out in the lounge where our big screen TVs run a continuous slideshow about our park, or just sit back and listen to D.J. Jazz play your favorite tunes.

10.   Add additional text and/or graphic images that will help to enhance the look and appearance of the outside left panel of the brochure.

11.   On the **Inside Left Panel** of the brochure, include the following:

- HOURS OF OPERATION:
  Monday-Friday   3 pm - 10 pm
  Saturday   9 am - 10 pm
  Sunday   9 am - 8 pm
  (Hours change during school vacations and summer - call 1-888-555-7245)

- MEMBERSHIP PLANS:
  Platinum: $800
  Full year unlimited skate or rollerblade, all day, includes 20% discount
  in the Pro Shop and free admission into special events
  Gold: $500
  Half a year unlimited skate or rollerblade, all day, includes 10% discount
  in the Pro Shop and free admission into special events
  Silver: $175
  Six months of skate or rollerblade for $8.00 per day, all day
  Bronze: $100
  Three months of skate or rollerblade for $8.00 per day, all day
  (During competition events, the park may be unavailable for short periods of time.)

- NON-MEMBER RATES:
  Monday—Thursday
  $12 for 6 hours
  Friday, Saturday & Sunday
  $15 for 6 hours

12. Add additional text and/or graphic images that will help to enhance the look and appearance of the inside left panel of the brochure.

13. On the **Inside Middle Panel** of the brochure, include the following:

   - RENTAL INFORMATION:
     Lockers $5/month
     Boards and Blades $2/hour
     Safety Gear (full set) $5/day

   - BIRTHDAY PARTIES:
     Celebrate your birthday at Skateboards, Inc.
     Party includes:
     4-hour session
     Helmet and Pad rentals
     Skateboard Shack Pizza
     Goodie Bags
     Your choice of music with D.J. Jazz
     Pricing:
     $12 per person/8 person minimum
     Parties over 10—birthday person FREE
     $20 deposit required 1 week prior to party
     WAIVERS FOR ALL PARTICIPANTS MUST BE ON FILE ONE WEEK PRIOR TO PARTY

14. Add additional text and/or graphic images that will help to enhance the look and appearance of the inside middle panel of the brochure.

15. On the **Inside Right Panel** of the brochure, include the following special information about Skateboards, Inc.:

   IMPORTANT SAFETY AND PARK INFORMATION:
   - Everyone who skates at Skateboards, Inc. must have a signed waiver on file with us.
   - Participants under the age of 18 must have their parent/guardian with proper ID sign the waiver in the presence of a Skate Park employee.
   - Everyone must wear a helmet at all times (participants over 18 must wear a helmet, but elbow and knee pads are optional).
   - Skateboards, Inc. sponsors "Lock Ins" every other month on Friday evenings. During these events, participants must arrive before 9 pm or they are locked out! Once in,

all participants are safely kept "locked up" until 8 am Saturday morning. This is a night jam-packed with fun (see Customer Service for more information).

- Gift cards are now available in our Pro Shop.
- Check our Web site at www.skateboardsinc.net for a complete up-to-date calendar of events.
- Private lessons are $25 per person or $40 for two (see Customer Service for more information).

16. Add additional text and/or graphic images that will help to enhance the look and appearance of the inside right panel of the brochure.

17. Carefully proofread your work for accuracy and format.

18. Resave the file.

19. Print a copy of the document if required by your instructor.
    Suggested: Print both sides of the brochure on one page and fold in thirds.

Create and Design a Boarder Birthday Pass (Extra Credit)

New Skills: Creating and Designing a Birthday Pass

TASK AND PURPOSE:

Create and design a Boarder Birthday Pass to be given to each member of Skateboards, Inc. The pass invites the member to bring a friend to skate for free on the member's birthday.

OVERVIEW:

When a new membership is purchased, the clerk will complete a Boarder Birthday Pass and present it to the member. All the member has to do then is decide which friend to invite when his or her birthday rolls around!

STRATEGIES AND TIPS TO CONSIDER:

1. Since the size of the pass (4 inches square) does not offer much display room, the design needs to be carefully planned.

2. The member name and birth date will be manually inserted, so be sure to allow enough space when you insert the lines.

3. Plan the layout and design of your birthday pass on paper first.

4. Read through all instructions before proceeding with the project.

INSTRUCTIONS, INFORMATION, AND REQUIRED CONTENT:

1. Before continuing, note that the layout, design, and fonts for this project will be left for you to decide.

2. Using Microsoft Publisher, or an equivalent desktop publishing software, create a new document.

3. Save the document as **Project P-8 Boarder Birthday Pass** in your "Publisher Projects" folder under your "Skateboards, Inc. Simulation" folder.

4. Set the page size to 8.5 inches wide x 11 inches tall with a 1 inch margin on all sides.

5. Using the rectangle tool, create a square that is 4 inches wide x 4 inches tall with a 1 point border. Place this square in the center of your document as shown in **Figure P-8-1**. Place the contents of the Boarder Birthday Pass within this border.

Figure P-8-1

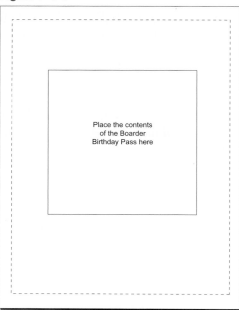

6. Insert the Skateboards, Inc. logo installed from the Skateboards, Inc. Resource CD. Resize the logo so it is in proportion with the rest of your document.

7. Include the following headline beneath the logo:

    Boarder Birthday Pass

8. Inside a rectangular border, include the following text as shown below. Add thin lines above the member's name and birth date, also shown below.

In honor of your birthday, we invite you to bring a friend to skate with you FREE OF CHARGE as our guest on your birthday!

_____

Member Name

_____

Member Birth Date
Happy Birthday!

9. Include a graphic image, such as a birthday cake, on the boarder pass.

10. Carefully proofread your work for accuracy and format.

11. Resave the file.

12. Print a copy of the document if required by your instructor.

SKATEBOARDS, INC.

PART 5:
POWERPOINT

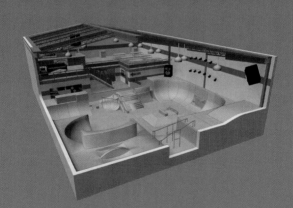

Create a Grand Opening Slide Show Presentation

New Skills: Applying Backgrounds • Applying Slide Transitions • Inserting Sound Files
• Applying Continuous Looping • Using Custom Animation • Using Bullets
• Printing Slides in Handout View • Presenting a Slide Show

TASK AND PURPOSE:

Create a PowerPoint presentation to run on the big screen TVs at Skateboards, Inc. during the Grand Opening Celebration and several weeks thereafter. The PowerPoint presentation will showcase all of the key features of Skateboards, Inc.

OVERVIEW:

Skateboards, Inc. is preparing to open its doors soon. The Grand Opening celebration is just around the corner, and Mr. Boardman has asked you to prepare a PowerPoint presentation to welcome people to Skateboards, Inc. The presentation will showcase features of Skateboards, Inc., such as a state-of-the-art facility, the Skateboard Shack Food Court, D.J. booth, Arcade, Pro Shop, the lounge, and much more.

STRATEGIES AND TIPS TO CONSIDER:

1. Be sure to use consistent design and typestyle elements throughout your presentation.

2. Each slide in your presentation should contain a consistent headline style.

3. Use graphic images that are consistent in style and help illustrate the text on each slide.

4. Be sure to include the Skateboards, Inc. logo on all slides.

5. Plan the layout and design of your Grand Opening Slide Show Presentation on paper first.

6. Read through all instructions before proceeding with the project.

INSTRUCTIONS, INFORMATION, AND REQUIRED CONTENT:

1. Before continuing, note that the layout, design, and fonts for this project will be left for you to decide.

2. Using Microsoft PowerPoint, create a new blank presentation.

3. Save the document as **Project PPT-1 Grand Opening Presentation** in your "PowerPoint Projects" folder under your "Skateboards, Inc. Simulation" folder.

4.   Before continuing, note the following requirements for this project and plan accordingly.

☒ All slides must include a consistent background
☒ All slides must include the Skateboards, Inc. logo
☐ One slide must contain the 3-D Sky View image of Skateboards, Inc.
☐ The slide show must contain a minimum of 11 slides
☐ Apply an identical slide transition throughout the presentation
☐ Upon completion, the slide show should be set up to loop continuously
☐ Insert a sound on at least three slides (optional)
☐ Apply custom animation to a minimum of three objects within the slide show

5.   On **slide 1**, include the following:

• Slide headline:
  Welcome to the Grand Opening of Skateboards, Inc.

• Slide sub headline:
  Rapid City's Latest and Greatest Skateboard and Rollerblade Park!

• The Skateboards, Inc. address and contact information:
  360 Jackson Boulevard
  Rapid City, SD 57702
  1-888-555-RAIL (7245)
  www.skateboardsinc.net

• The following text:
  Presentation Designed by
  <Your Name>,
  Skateboards, Inc. Microsoft Office Specialist

• Add additional text and/or graphic images that you feel will help illustrate and enhance the content and appearance of the slide.

6.   On **slide 2**, include the following:

• Slide headline:
  A Message from Randy Boardman, President

• Under the headline compose a 3-5 sentence welcome message to "Fellow Boarders" welcoming them to Skateboards, Inc. The message should "thank" customers for choosing Skateboards, Inc. and encourage them to find out more about the park by visiting a Skateboards, Inc. employee. Note in the message that employees of Skateboards, Inc. will be wearing red t-shirts and name badges, making them easy to identify.

7.   On **slide 3**, include the following:

• Slide headline:
  About Skateboards, Inc.

• Under the headline, place a brief, one paragraph summary about Skateboards, Inc.
  Tip: Refer to "Project W-1: Write a Press Release" to help you write your summary.

• A bullet list of key features and highlights of Skateboards, Inc.

• Add additional text and/or graphic images that you feel will help illustrate and enhance the content and appearance of the slide.

8.   On **slide 4**, include the following:

• Slide headline:
  Hours of Operation

• Under the headline, list the hours of operation of the park.
  Tip: Copy and paste the "Hours of Operation" by retrieving "Project W-8: Hours of Operation."

• Add additional text and/or graphic images that you feel will help illustrate and enhance the content and appearance of the slide.

9.   On **slide 5**, include the following:

• Slide headline:
  Visit The Skateboard Shack

• Under the headline, highlight and describe some of the best items included in The Skateboard Shack menu.
  Tip: Refer to "Project P-6: Create and Design a Booklet-Style Food Menu" for a list of menu items.

• Add additional text and/or graphic images that you feel will help illustrate and enhance the content and appearance of the slide.

10.   On **slide 6**, include the following:

• Slide headline:
  Music Provided By D.J. Jazz

• Under the headline, include two or three features and highlights of the D.J. booth.
  Example: "Stop by and talk to D.J. Jazz and ask him to play your favorite song."
  Tip: Refer to "Project E-3: Create a Music List" to assist you with this task.

- Add additional text and/or graphic images that you feel will help illustrate and enhance the content and appearance of the slide.

11. On **slide 7**, include the following:

- Slide headline:
  Visit the Skateboards, Inc. Pro Shop

- Under the headline, list some of the equipment that is available at the Pro Shop.
  Tip: Refer to Project "E-6: Create a Pro Shop Equipment Inventory Report" to assist you.

- Add additional text and/or graphic images that you feel will help illustrate and enhance the content and appearance of the slide.

12. On **slide 8**, include the following:

- Slide headline:
  Experience Gaming in the Skateboards, Inc. Arcade

- Under the headline, include the following list of categories and games available in the Skateboards, Inc. Arcade:

Pinball Machines:	Video Games:	Sports Table Games:	Other:
Olympic Ski Racer	Money Chase!	Foosball	Photo Booth
Monsters from the Deep	Arachnids	Soccer	Skee-Ball Alley
Speed-Racer	Bowl-away	Football	Pool Table
Star-Blaster!	Zoom!		
Martians & Moonmen	Tornado Alley		
Truckin'	War Zone		

- Add additional text and/or graphic images that you feel will help illustrate and enhance the content and appearance of the slide.

13. On **slide 9**, include the following:

- Slide headline:
  Take a Breather in The Lounge

- Under the headline, write a brief description of the lounge area and the fact that it is a comfortable, quiet place to discuss skateboarding strategies with friends while enjoying a snack and viewing what is being played on the big screen TVs.

- Add additional text and/or graphic images that you feel will help illustrate and enhance the content and appearance of the slide.

14. On **slide 10**, include the following:

- Slide headline:
  Affordable Memberships Available

- Under the headline, include the following text:

  Stop by our membership desk and check out the following plans:

  PLATINUM MEMBERSHIP: $800
  Includes one year unlimited skate or rollerblade, all day, includes 20% discount on all items available in the Pro Shop and free admission into special events

  GOLD: $500
  Half a year unlimited skate or rollerblade, all day, includes 10% discount on all items available in the Pro Shop and free admission into special events

  SILVER: $175
  Six months of skate or rollerblade for $8.00 per day, all day

  BRONZE: $100
  Three months of skate or rollerblade for $8.00 per day, all day

- Add additional text and/or graphic images that you feel will help illustrate and enhance the content and appearance of the slide.

15. On **slide 11**, include the following:

- Slide headline:
  Safety Is Our #1 Priority

- Under the headline, include the following heading and bullet list:

  For a safe "boarding" and "blading" experience, follow these safety tips:
  - Always wear a helmet.
  - Always wear protective elbow and knee pads.
  - Never bring food or beverage into the skate arena.
  - Be respectful of fellow boarders and bladers.
  - Always use caution on rails and ramps.
  - Know your limitations: beginners should avoid risky moves.

- Add additional text and/or graphic images that you feel will help illustrate and enhance the content and appearance of the slide.

16. *Optional*: Insert one additional slide that includes more details about Skateboards, Inc. that you feel are noteworthy.

17.   Carefully review the list of project requirements provided in **Step 4**. Be sure that you have met each requirement.

18.   Carefully proofread your work for accuracy and format.

19.   Resave the file.

20.   Print out a copy of your presentation as handouts using four slides per page if required by your instructor.

21.   If you are required to present your slide show, review the "PowerPoint Presentation Tips" provided below to help you prepare.

PowerPoint Presentation Tips

- Speak slowly and clearly when presenting
- Use transitions that match your topic
- Make no more than six points per slide
- Have a classmate proofread and critique your presentation before you present it
- Use no more than two to three fonts throughout your presentation
- Rehearse your presentation before delivering it to your audience
- Choose a consistent, professional design and color scheme that is easy-on-the-eyes
- Keep the style of graphic images consistent throughout the presentation
- Do not clutter each slide within your presentation
- Use sounds and animation to bring content to life, but do not overuse them
- Prepare notes to help you deliver an effective and dynamic presentation

Create a Banner Advertising Campaign Presentation (Extra Credit)

New Skills: Inserting a Table • Formatting Tables

TASK AND PURPOSE:

Create a PowerPoint presentation that provides information to local business owners about the banner advertising campaign available at Skateboards, Inc.

OVERVIEW:

Marketing Director Rebecca Langford is developing an advertising campaign directed at local business owners giving them the opportunity to advertise their businesses on banners of various sizes and colors to hang from the rafters or be displayed on side walls at Skateboards, Inc.
An informational packet introducing the advertising campaign will be mailed to prospective advertisers. After the mailing, Rebecca will contact the potential advertisers to set up an appointment to go over the campaign. Your role is to design the PowerPoint presentation to be presented by Rebecca to the prospective advertisers at their individual meetings.

STRATEGIES AND TIPS TO CONSIDER:

1. Be sure to use consistent design and typestyle elements throughout your presentation.

2. Each slide in your presentation should contain a consistent headline style.

3. Use graphic images that are consistent in style and help illustrate the text on each slide.

4. Be sure to include the Skateboards, Inc. logo on all slides.

5. Plan the layout and design of your Banner Advertising Campaign Presentation on paper first.

6. Read through all instructions before proceeding with the project.

INSTRUCTIONS, INFORMATION, AND REQUIRED CONTENT:

1. Before continuing, note that the layout, design, and fonts for this project will be left for you to decide.

2. Using Microsoft PowerPoint, create a new blank presentation.

3. Save the document as **Project PPT-2 Banner Advertising Campaign Presentation** in your "PowerPoint Projects" folder under your "Skateboards, Inc. Simulation" folder.

4. Before continuing, note the following requirements for this project and plan accordingly.

    ☐ All slides must include the Skateboards, Inc. logo
    ☐ One slide must contain the 3-D Sky View image of Skateboards, Inc.
    ☐ The slide show must contain a minimum of six slides
    ☐ Apply an identical slide transition to each slide that advances to the next slide when the user clicks the mouse
    ☐ Insert a sound on at least three slides (optional)
    ☐ Apply custom animation to a minimum of at least three objects within the slide show

5. On **slide 1**, include the following:

    • Slide headline:
      Introducing Skateboards, Inc. Banner Advertising Campaign

    • The following text:
      Presentation Designed by
      <Your Name>,
      Skateboards, Inc. Microsoft Office Specialist

    • Add additional text and/or graphic images that you feel will help illustrate and enhance the content and appearance of the slide.

6. On **slide 2**, include the following:

    • Slide headline:
      Why Advertise at Skateboards, Inc.?

    • Under the headline, insert the following information in bullet list format:

      • Advertising attracts new customers
      • Advertising encourages repeat business
      • Advertising keeps you in the competitive race
      • Advertising keeps your business top-of-mind
      • Advertising gives your business a successful image

    • Add additional text and/or graphic images that you feel will help illustrate and enhance the content and appearance of the slide.

7.   On **slide 3**, include the following:

• Slide headline:
How the Advertising Program Works

• Under the headline, insert the following information in bullet list format:

• You choose the size, color scheme, and background design of your banner
• Banners will be created, designed, and printed by Canvas Creations, Inc.
• Pricing is based on the banner size and placement within our facility
• Banners will be hung from various rafters and displayed on side walls throughout the skate park

• Under the bullet list, create and place a sample banner advertisement image similar to the one shown in **Figure PPT-2-1**.

Figure PPT-2-1

• Under the sample banner advertisement image, add the following caption:
Sample Banner Advertisement

• Add additional text and/or graphic images that you feel will help illustrate and enhance the content and appearance of the slide.

8.   On **slide 4**, include the following:

• Slide headline:
Banner Advertisement Options

• Under the headline, insert a table with 4 columns and 5 rows and key in the information as it appears in **Figure PPT-2-2**.
Note: Merge column and row cells in the table as they appear in Figure PPT-2-2.

• Add additional text and/or graphic images that you feel will help illustrate and enhance the content and appearance of the slide.

Figure PPT-2-2

Size	Color	Background	Price
Small Pole Sleeve (19.5" high x 14" wide)	Color scheme and designs are limited to the selection you have received in your handout	Choose one of the following: solid color, patriotic, festive, pinstripes, or clouds (most popular), or choose one from your enclosed handout	$39.95*
Medium Pole Sleeve (31" high x 22.25" wide)			$59.95*
Large Pole Sleeve (42" high x 30" wide)			$79.95*
All banners include banner pole and hang cord. When your advertising contract is completed, the banner will be taken down and delivered to your business address. *Pricing is for letter banners only – an additional charge will be added for logos or any other photo on banner.			

9. On **slide 5**, include the following:

    • Slide headline:
      Advertising Pricing Options

    • Under the headline, insert a table with 6 columns and 5 rows and key in the information as it appears in **Figure PPT-2-3**.
      Note: Merge the cells in the bottom row.

    • Add additional text and/or graphic images that you feel will help illustrate and enhance the content and appearance of the slide.

Figure PPT-2-3

Small Banner	Price	Medium Banner	Price	Large Banner	Price
1-2 months*	$39.95	1-2 months*	$59.95	1-2 months*	$79.95
3-6 months*	$129.95	3-6 months*	$149.95	3-6 months*	$169.95
7-12 months*	$199.95	7-12 months*	$249.95	7-12 months*	$299.95
*indicates amount of time the banner will be on display					

10. On **slide 6**, include the following:

    • Slide headline:
      Advertising with Skateboards, Inc. Makes Sense

    • Under the headline, insert the following text:

      Thank you for taking the time to view this presentation. We hope you will consider advertising at Skateboards, Inc. If we can be of further assistance, please contact us at 1-888-555-RAIL (7245).

    • Add additional text and/or graphic images that you feel will help illustrate and enhance the content and appearance of the slide.

11. *Optional*: Insert an additional slide that includes more details that will attract businesses to advertise at Skateboards, Inc.

12. Carefully review the list of project requirements provided in **Step 4**. Be sure that you have met each requirement.

13. Carefully proofread your work for accuracy and format.

14. Resave the file.

15. Print out a copy of your presentation as handouts using four slides per page if required by your instructor.

16. If you are required to present your slide show, review the "PowerPoint Presentation Tips" provided at the conclusion of Project PPT-1.